Subtle Insights Concerning Knowledge and Practice

World Thought in Translation

A joint project of Yale University Press and the MacMillan Center for International and Area Studies at Yale University, World Thought in Translation makes important works of classical and contemporary political, philosophical, legal, and social thought from outside the Western tradition available to English-speaking scholars, students, and general readers. The translations are annotated and accompanied by critical introductions that orient readers to the background in which these texts were written, their initial reception, and their enduring influence within and beyond their own cultures. World Thought in Translation contributes to the study of religious and secular intellectual traditions across cultures and civilizations.

Series editors

Stephen Angle
Andrew March
Ian Shapiro

Subtle Insights Concerning Knowledge and Practice

Kalimāt wajīza mushtamila ʻalā nukat laṭīfa fī al-ʻilm wa-l-ʻamal

Saʻd ibn Mansur Ibn Kammūna al-Baghdādī

Translated, with an Introduction and Commentary, by Y. Tzvi Langermann

Yale UNIVERSITY PRESS
New Haven and London

This publication was made possible in part by a grant from the Carnegie Corporation of New York. The statements made and views expressed are solely the responsibility of the author.

The author acknowledges with gratitude the support of the Israel Science Foundation, Grant 279/13.

Published with assistance from the Mary Cady Tew Memorial Fund.

Yale University Press books may be purchased in quantity for educational, business, or promotional use. For information, please e-mail sales.press@yale.edu (U.S. office) or sales@yaleup.co.uk (U.K. office).

Set in Adobe Caslon type by Newgen North America, Austin, Texas.
Printed in the United States of America.

Library of Congress Control Number: 2019932776
ISBN 978-0-300-20369-1 (hardcover : alk. paper)

A catalogue record for this book is available from the British Library.

This paper meets the requirements of ANSI/NISO Z39.48-1992 (Permanence of Paper).

10 9 8 7 6 5 4 3 2 1

Contents

Subtle Insights
Concerning Knowledge
and Practice

Translator's Introduction

The few facts that we possess concerning Ibn Kammūna's biography leave open many questions concerning the book whose translation I place before the reader, a short book with a long title: *Kalimāt wajīza mushtamila 'alā nukat laṭīfa fī al-'ilm wa-l-'amal,* literally "Brief Words Containing Nice Points Concerning Knowledge and Practice."[1] Though he does carry the surname al-Baghdādī, Ibn Kammūna's birthplace, and birthdate, are both unknown.[2] His only attested journey is his flight from Baghdad late in life to Hilla, where he died. I have presented evidence for his presence in Aleppo, but that feature of his biography does not bear upon the *Kalimāt.*[3] In 1268 Ibn Kammūna records his presence in "Iraq"; his biographers Reza Pourjavady and Sabine Schmidtke take this to refer to Baghdad.[4] His working life was spent almost entirely in the area of Baghdad, then under pagan Mongol rule.

Ibn Kammūna's network included two major scholars of his day, both Muslims.[5] He corresponded with Naṣīr al-Dīn al-Ṭūsī, an outstanding astronomer, mathematician, and philosopher, and someone quite close to the seat of Mongol power.[6] Al-Ṭūsī's relationship with Ibn Kammūna does not look to me to have been particularly close. By contrast, it seems that Ibn Kammūna was on more intimate terms with the philosopher and logician Najm al-Dīn al-Kātibī.[7] Each of them dedicated a work to the same member of the powerful Juwaynī clan, and they probably shared the same patron.[8] As far as we know al-Kātibī is the only correspondent whom Ibn Kammūna met in person. Ibn Kammūna commented on al-Kātibī's criticisms of the theologian Fakhr al-Dīn al-Rāzī's *al-Ma'ālim fī Uṣūl al-Dīn* (Signposts in the Principles of the Religion)—an unusual excursion into Muslim *kalam* (scholastic theology) for a Jewish writer.[9] Ibn Kammūna also corresponded with a Shi'ite scholar, Maytham al-Bahrānī. Al-Kātibī may well have served as the link connecting Ibn Kammūna to the leading circle of scholars of his day. Pourjavady and Schmidtke tellingly remark that it was Ibn Kammūna who took the initiative in all these correspondences. On the other hand, Ibn Kammūna was approached by the historian Ibn al-Fuwaṭī in 1280–1281, shortly before his demise.[10]

We know that Ibn Kammūna held some sort of position in the service of the Mongols, and that his patron was the Ṣāḥib al-Dīwān, or treasurer, Shams al-Dīn al-Juwaynī. However, we do not know what office Ibn Kammūna held, and to what extent his office required, or allowed, him to make contact with the many people of highly variegated backgrounds who made up the Mongol court. Presumably he was involved in the administrative apparatus set up by al-Juwaynī in Baghdad, which was busily, and successfully, restoring a functioning and flourishing economy to the metropolis after the ravages of the Mongol conquest. All of Ibn Kammūna's correspondents, other than Ibn al-Fuwaṭī, were part of al-Ṭūsī's circle of scholars at Maragha, located in what is now the Iranian province of East Azerbaijan.[11] Did he travel with the Mongol court in their sojourns to the Azerbaijan steppes? If he was not at court, then did he spend any time at Maragha, famous for its observatory but also home to an important madrasa where philosophical texts were studied? Pourjavady and Schmidtke do not rule out a visit to Maragha, despite the lack of any evidence.[12] Be that as it may, Ibn Kammūna has left some footprints in Maragha, particularly in the library of the astronomer, medical writer, and philosopher Quṭb al-Dīn al-Shīrāzī.[13] We do not know whether Ibn Kammūna knew or met Rashīd al-Dīn al-Hamdhānī, the vizier to the khans Ghazan and Öljeitü, or Rashīd al-Dīn's father and/or grandfather. Rashīd al-Dīn too was a Jew in the service of the Mongols, though he converted to Islam; his interests were far-ranging, including philosophy and religion. Unlike his famous world history, Rashīd al-Dīn's many short treatises on science and philosophy have hardly been touched by academic scholarship.[14] In any event, a codex containing some of Ibn Kammūna's writings was in the personal library of Rashīd al-Dīn.[15]

Several of Ibn Kammūna's works were written for government officials. His major work, *al-Jadīd fī al-Ḥikma* (New Wisdom), completed in 1278, was written for Dawlatshāh b. Sanjar al-Ṣāḥibī, who was a government official and may also have been a student of Ibn Kammūna's. Pourjavady and Schmidtke presume that Dawlatshāh was highly placed and working in Baghdad at the time.[16] The *Kalimāt*, completed in the following year, was written for Bahā' al-Dīn al-Juwaynī, son of Shams al-Dīn al-Juwaynī, while Bahā' al-Dīn was staying in Baghdad.[17]

The *Kalimāt* is meant to contain in capsular form Ibn Kammūna's "discourse on intellectual matters (*ʿaqliyyāt*)." He includes in it "nice points concerning knowledge and practice" (*nukat laṭīfa fī al-ʿilm wa-l-ʿamal*) which he organized symmetrically: two "gates," or sets of "points," on knowledge and two on practice. The sections on knowledge deal with knowledge of the deity, or the "Necessary Existent," and knowledge of the soul—which amounts to a person's knowledge of his own self. The first section on practice concerns personal ethics, the second political matters—that is, advice on how to govern.

The metaphysics or theology of the *Kalimāt* is by and large along the lines of the philosophy expounded by Ibn Kammūna in his encyclopedic *al-Jadīd fī al-Ḥikma* (New Wisdom), and, perhaps to a lesser extent, the same holds for the section on the soul. I say to a lesser extent because Ibn Kammūna, who was obsessed with the soul's endless perdurance, never tired of devising more and more proofs for this doctrine, and in the *Kalimāt* he has some new things to say on the matter. The second half, on *ʿamal* or praxis, covers issues of self-control and interpersonal relations, as well as politics. With regard to personal conduct Ibn Kammūna urges basically an otherworldly approach, much in line with Sufi teachings. Some passages are copied almost verbatim from Sufi writings of the twelfth-century philosopher and mystic Shihāb al-Dīn al-Suhrawardī, whose philosophical writings were a major influence on Ibn Kammūna.[18] The "mirror for princes" which makes up the second section reveals a new side to Ibn Kammūna's interests.

An even shorter treatise by Ibn Kammūna, *Ithbāt al-Mabda'* (Establishing the Origin), reproduces almost word for word sections of the *Kalimāt;* it is not clear which was written first.[19]

Ibn Kammūna's *Tanqīḥ* (Examination), a critical comparison of Judaism, Islam, and Christianity, and his most famous writing, is helpful for understanding the *Kalimāt.*[20] The *Kalimāt* must have been completed by December 1279, and the *Tanqīḥ* by October 1280.[21] It seems likely, then, that the two works were on Ibn Kammūna's worktable at the same time. He must have been involved in his researches for the *Tanqīḥ* while writing the *Kalimāt.* From the *Tanqīḥ* we learn that Ibn Kammūna made a close study of the three faiths. Even if he had the aim of defending Judaism against polemicists like the twelfth-century apostate and author of a severe attack on Judaism, Samaw'al al-Maghribī, the *Tanqīḥ* is far more than a defense.[22] Before beginning his comparison, which perforce highlights the differences among the three faiths, Ibn Kammūna presents a chapter on prophecy, an institution which serves as the foundation of all three. Three Muslim authorities who are utilized are cited by name—the physician, astronomer, and philosopher Ibn Sīnā (Avicenna); the philosopher, jurist, and theologian al-Ghazālī; and the theologian and philosopher Fakhr al-Dīn al-Rāzī—but only one Jewish one, the astronomer, physician, and philosopher Moses Maimonides. Ibn Kammūna's acquaintance with Jewish sources certainly went beyond the basic biblical education we can presume that he received, and his study of Muslim and Christian literature extended far beyond the norm among Jews of his epoch.

Moshe Perlmann has shown that the section of the *Tanqīḥ* which presents Judaism relies on both Maimonides and Yehuda ha-Levi's *Cuzari;* the blending of Maimonides with ha-Levi appears strange to contemporary academic sensibilities, but it is by no means unique to Ibn Kammūna.[23] In the section on Christianity Ibn Kammūna takes care to cite what he calls the Christian version of biblical texts; this is a sensitivity to different traditions concerning the same text that one does not meet with frequently. He maintains all along a reverential attitude towards Jesus. Perlmann observes that this chapter indicates that Ibn Kammūna did not consider Christianity to be a serious threat, the successes of the Nestorians under the Mongols notwithstanding. However, there are some passages in the *Kalimāt* that may be viewed as a jibe against the Christians. These appear in Ibn Kammūna's effort to arrive at a pure monotheism, which cannot allow trinitarianism. The section of the *Tanqīḥ* on Islam is far longer than the one given to Christianity. Ibn Kammūna's close study of Islam is well attested from his notes to al-Kātibī; the *Tanqīḥ* displays again his reliance on Fakhr al-Dīn al-Rāzī.

Moshe Perlmann notes further that, in the *Tanqīḥ*, "Jewish tenets (e.g., of Maimonides) are de-judaized, Islamic tenets (e.g., statements by Ghazālī, Avicenna) are de-islamicized in the attempt to reach the common denominator of human beliefs, attitudes, institutions."[24] In my opinion, the research that Ibn Kammūna put into that book played a key role in the development of his personal Abrahamic monotheism; in particular, his studies equipped him with the tools to craft the *Kalimāt*, most notably with regard to its judicial choice of references from the Qur'an and hadith. For example, one of the rare scriptural quotations in the *Kalimāt*, occurring in the first of the four sections, is the Qur'anic verse "He is the First and the Last, the Apparent and the Hidden" ("Iron," 57:3); the same verse is found in Isaiah 48:12 and Revelation 1:8. This can be no coincidence; Ibn Kammūna's knowledge of all three traditions allowed him to select precisely an identical textual support found in all three. As an open-minded thinker working at the Ilkhanid court, Ibn Kammūna would most likely have been exposed to Buddhist thought as well. I believe that some traces of this influence are also present in the *Kalimāt,* and I discuss them in the Synopsis and Commentary sections, especially to the last section of the book.

The political ethos of the Ilkhanid rule was certainly congenial to religious toleration. ʿAlāʾ al-Juwaynī, the historian and brother of Ibn Kammūna's patron, lauded his overlords for the respect that they showed to "the learned and pious of every sect, recognising such conduct as the way to the Court of God." Though members of the imperial household had chosen different religions for themselves, according to the historian George Lane, "They still for the most part avoid all show of fanaticism and do not swerve from the *yasa* of Chinggis Khan, namely, to consider all sects as one and not to distinguish them from one another."[25] Lane's assessment is by and large substantiated in the recent comprehensive study of Peter Jackson.[26] Moreover, Lane notes that al-Juwaynī "saw the Mongols' recognition of One God as not incompatible with his own faith in the One God."[27] The same can be said of Ibn Kammūna, certainly with regard to Muslims; in his case the harmony of monotheism is firmly established philosophically in all of his writings. Whatever political benefits his views may have conferred, I am convinced that the "Abrahamic" monotheism of Ibn Kammūna was a sincere belief and the product of years of study and contemplation. His inclusion of traditional Muslim encomia on the Prophet in his books is no more evidence for his conversion to Islam than his reverential attitude towards Jesus testifies to a conversion to Christianity. Indeed, his remarks concerning the reasons why Jews convert to Islam—reasons that have little to do with belief or rational arguments—argue forcefully against his own conversion.[28] Conversion would certainly not be required for salvation, which rests in realizing the values set forth in this treatise. It is available for anyone willing to make the effort to achieve it.

Nonetheless, fanaticism and intolerance were certainly present. The question of the situation within Isfahan—the city whose rule the patron of the *Kalimāt* was about to assume—is made all the more intriguing by Ibn Kammūna's forceful, and original, warning to respect the *dhimmīs* in particular. "For this reason the 'people of experience' (*arbāb al-tajārib*) say, 'Harming the *dhimma* people [leads to the removal of] the king and removes good fortune.' This is not limited to them, but rather [extends] to every victim who has no one to help him."[29] As a Jew, of course, Ibn Kammūna would have a vested interest in tolerance. But are his remarks directed more specifically at local issues that Bahā' al-Dīn would be expected to face in Isfahan, which had somehow come to the attention of Ibn Kammūna? Or were they included because the *Kalimāt* was intended to be a vade mecum not just for Bahā' al-Dīn, but for all rulers, wherever they may govern? At present I have no answer to these questions.

Another set of questions concerns Bahā' al-Dīn and his newly assigned outpost, Isfahan. How well did Ibn Kammūna know Bahā' al-Dīn, if at all?[30] To what extent was the *Kalimāt* tailored to his personality, temperament, and presumed style of government? Again, I have no information on these points. Clearly, they press mainly on the fourth and final section of the *Kalimāt,* which deals with political leadership and governance. The first part, on *'ilm* (knowledge or science), is, for all its brevity, not a text that a novice can understand with ease, if at all. Indeed, parts of it are challenging even to specialists. Bahā' al-Dīn is reported to have devoted some time to learned discussions and to have patronized scholars, poets, and artists; perhaps Ibn Kammūna had reason to believe that he would have been able to appreciate its contents. In any event, the book was intended mainly for the library of Bahā' al-Dīn, and Ibn Kammūna would not have been the first to write a text whose true audience was not confined to its designated patron.

We do not know much about Bahā' al-Dīn, but he seems to have been a very harsh ruler. True, even mild-mannered people may undergo a change of behavior when given absolute power. Isfahan may have been Bahā' al-Dīn's first appointment, and Ibn Kammūna may not have known what to expect. Perhaps crime and disorder were rampant there, and their suppression may, in keeping with the mores of the time, have justified severe measures. Even so, his father, Ṣāḥib al-Dīwān Shams al-Dīn al-Juwaynī, wrote to his son, warning him against the brutality that had reached his ears. The historian Wassāf reports that Bahā' al-Dīn ignored his father's advice, but he also relates that after Bahā' al-Dīn's death in 1279, crime was again rampant in Isfahan. The severity of Bahā' al-Dīn's rule was accepted, it appears, by his contemporaries. Even so, Bahā' al-Dīn is portrayed as a man possessed of an inhuman cruelty, which can be neither explained nor, indeed, fathomed. What are we to think of someone who orders the execution of his favorite son for playfully grasping at his beard? I will not indulge in the sort of revisionism that banishes unpalatable stories to legend.

My translation is based upon the edition of the Arabic text of the *Kalimāt* published by Reza Pourjavady and Sabine Schmidtke in *A Jewish Philosopher of Baghdad: 'Izz al-Dawla Ibn Kammuna (d. 683/1284) and His Writings* (Leiden: Brill, 2006), with thanks to Brill Publishers. I do not have access to any of the five manuscripts which Pourjavady and Schmidtke used. However, I am satisfied that their edition is a good one, including the rich listings of variants in the footnotes; on not a few occasions I have chosen one of the variant readings which they display. These occurrences are all recorded in my notes to the translation. Only once or twice have I been unable to make sense of any of the readings and been forced to suggest a minor emendation.

In the course of decades of translating philosophical and scientific texts from Arabic and Hebrew into English I have performed a delicate balancing act. My assignment as I see it is twofold: to fathom as best I can what the author intends to say in his book, and then to get this message across as clearly as I can in English. I must, of course, adhere as closely as possible to the literal meaning of the text in the source language—a need only exacerbated by the phobia that a highly trained, and perhaps overly pedantic, Arabist is looking over my shoulder, gently prodding that "this is not precisely what the Arabic says." However, my responsibility to the English language, and its own literary standards, is no less weighty; indeed, since the Arabist presumably can read Ibn Kammūna without the benefit of my translation, those who cannot read the text in the original should be foremost in my mind. They deserve a translation designed to be comprehensible to the English reader rather than one aimed at pleasing the Arabophone specialist.

For this book I have chosen the following tack. I first present a synopsis and commentary for each of the four sections. The language is entirely my own; in writing the synopses, in particular, I thought only of how to get the message across in English as smoothly as possible. I include in the synopses detailed discussions of specific points raised in the texts, which in the accepted practice of past generations would have been put in very long footnotes. Obviously, this means that the reader is getting my interpretation of Ibn Kammūna—but that happens even in a literal translation. Having done this, I allow myself to present a translation that is more literal—meaning, inevitably, more stultified and heavy. Even so, the differences between the two languages force me to add words to the English in brackets in order to construct a comprehensible sentence. Page numbers to the edition of Pourjavady and Schmidtke are given in brackets in the translation; the number precedes the first word of the page in the edition. Notes to the translation are kept short and reserved for indicating my choice of a variant to the edition of Pourjavady and Schmidtke, various textual issues that cannot be ignored, and occasional brief clarifications.

I acknowledge here the support of the Israel Science Foundation, Grant 279/13, and the assistance of Dr. Leigh Chipman with the first draft of my translation.

PART I.
ON KNOWLEDGE
FIRST GATE

Synopsis and Commentary

The title of the first of the four sections (each called in Arabic *jumla*) introduces the Supreme Being. It is He whom we must know and worship. This being is given two names or designations: *mudabbir*, Governor (or Director, Administrator: the entity responsible for the orderly workings of the cosmos), and *wājib al-wujūd*, "that whose existence is necessary," a widely used philosophical description and appellation of the Supreme Being. Its full signification is subtle and subject to interpretation, but basically it means "the being that cannot not be." The term further implies that this being's existence is not contingent on any other.

The first chapter introduces the intended reader, who is a "seeker of knowledge," to the categories of knowledge, and these categories are given rankings. The ancients have already recorded everything; however, some say that they fully explicated only the general principles, leaving out the precise treatment of fine points. The ancients have only opened the doors and shown the way. Since that time, knowledge has grown to such an extent that no individual can encompass it all. In sum, the ancients did not—perhaps they could not—tell us everything; the seeker of perfection must make an informed choice concerning which subjects, which bodies of information, to master. The ancients opened the gates, but they did not close the book.

The reader is also told what true knowledge, or knowledge of the "true realities" (*al-ḥaqā'iq*), consists in. The second chapter, as we shall shortly see, essentially recapitulates the title of the entire section—hence it may be said to convey the pivotal information the section contains. But let us not get ahead of ourselves.

Ibn Kammūna notes that the soul has both a speculative and a practical faculty, and each has its own purpose: the former to attain knowledge, the latter to induce action. But the items of knowledge and action are many and ramified. The ancients have already recorded all the relevant details in their books, and Ibn Kammūna seems inclined towards the view that the ancients have left nothing to be added. Nonetheless, it has been said—and Ibn Kammūna does not reject this—that the ancients have settled only the principles. In so doing, they have opened for us "the gates of knowing." They have indeed left room for us to refine our knowledge of the finer points. In any event, given the tremendous scope of what must be mastered, it is best for "the seeker of perfection" to focus upon the things that are most important for both mundane and spiritual concerns.

This leads Ibn Kammūna to a fundamental statement concerning a consensus that encompasses all religions as well as all philosophies: in his words, "the masters of traditional religions as well as [the masters] of intellectual tenets" all agree upon it. The consensus covers three principles: belief in God (here he uses the proper name Allāh) and in the end of days, and doing good works. The same statement is found in the introduction to Ibn Kammūna's encyclopedic *New Wisdom* (*al-Jadid fī al-ḥikma).*[1] In his concise *Epitome of Wisdom* (*Talkhīṣ al-ḥikma*), Ibn Kammūna takes note of the consensus of the prophets and the "scholars who verify" with regard to a different list of three items. There, however, instead of the end of days, Ibn Kammūna mentions God's attributes; and instead of the need for humans to do good things, he names God's works.[2] The three items mentioned in our text—belief in God and in the end of days, and doing good works—are the first things to be ingested intellectually by the seeker of knowledge. From them the seeker will proceed to other matters, as Ibn Kammūna explains in the discourse which follows. Ibn Kammūna was certainly not alone in acknowledging the monotheism of the (Hellenistic) philosophers. Similar views are expressed by Miskawayh and al-Āmiri, to name just two other philosophers with whom Ibn Kammūna was certainly aligned ideologically even if he did not necessarily read their books.[3] However, I have not encountered as sweeping a statement as Ibn Kammūna's assertion of a consensus embracing philosophers and revealed religion. Refining our conception of the divine being requires us to contemplate the characteristics that are attributed to God by Scripture or in books on theology, and then to strip away attributes that ascribe to the deity, even indirectly, the slightest trace of materiality. This is the process of *tawḥīd,* literally "making [God] one."

Ibn Kammūna next delineates the progress of the seeker, whose goals are to know in particular the immateriality of the deity and His providential care; the human soul, especially her afterlife; and the practical issues of the soul's edification and avoidance of failure.

The reasons Ibn Kammūna gives as to why the intelligent person (*al-'āqil*) must know all this are surprising. Three options are presented, the exercise of each one of which requires the knowledge just described. Should the intellectual wish to deny the items that are agreed upon by "people of wisdom and revelation" (the consensus described above), he must back up his denial with sound arguments. Should he accept the consensually consented-to principles, he must still exert himself to acquire them as personal knowledge. In other words, these principles are not a catechism, to which a person simply declares allegiance, but items of knowledge which each person must make his or her own, must assimilate to his or her personality, by means of intellectual effort. Finally, should the intellectually astute seeker be unsure about whether these principles are true, it would certainly be "most prudent" to look into them deeply. Ibn Kammūna is not urging the doubtful reader to believe; instead he is counseling the avoidance of disbelief as a matter of caution. The "prudence" he advocates is of the sort now known as "Pascal's wager."[4] Ibn Kammūna does not promise an infinite reward if it happens that belief is justified. However, he hints that there is a great if not infinite punishment for those who choose disbelief. Plato avers that his lukewarm endorsement of the metensomatosis (a precise technical term for the migration of the soul into a new body) is a "reasonable contention and a belief worth risking, for the risk is a noble one. We should use such accounts to inspire ourselves with confidence" (*Phaedo* 114D). If we must look for a source, then Plato will surely do. However, I am not aware of anything like Ibn Kammūna's argument here in Islamic or Jewish sources.[5]

Though Ibn Kammūna adds parenthetically that accepting the consensus of beliefs is incumbent on us, his exposition gives the reader the sense that any of the three routes to its acceptance is legitimate and viable.

Of the two branches, knowledge and practice, the former is primary. However, true knowledge is not what most people think it to be. True knowledge consists (as I understand Ibn Kammūna) in what is superadded to routine knowledge (the sciences and disciplines, such as physics or medicine, that are learned from books and lectures) by means of insights into personal shortcomings. Ethical introspection upgrades knowledge acquired by the usual methods of study, and reinforces the lessening of one's desire for this-worldly affairs.

The intimate connection between wisdom and ethics, and the dependence of the acquisition of true knowledge on the loosening of our bonds to this world, call to mind the first exchange between the aspirant and Patanjali in al-Bīrūnī's Sufi-flavored reworking of the *Yogasutra.* The aspirant ascetic tells of his search for certain proofs about immaterial reality. Patanjali answers, "Your quest lies in practice," and then displays three different paths, all of which involve directing the mind away from the material universe.[6] The ethos is much the same, even though it is highly unlikely that Ibn Kammūna ever saw al-Bīrūnī's book.

Ibn Kammūna elaborates: True knowledge means knowledge of the Truth. It is goal directed, and the goal—the Truth—is divine and otherworldly. A life of study in which the mind is not oriented towards the deity is not a life well spent. Proper orientation is a constant worry; losing the proper focus drops the seeker into the ranks of "fools and ignoramuses." The reader is reminded that "Knowledge of the true reality is a wide ocean and a distant road." The information that Ibn Kammūna has packed into this small book, so he tells us, is the barest minimum and absolutely necessary even for those who do not complete the journey.

The opening paragraph of the second chapter furnishes a beautiful example of the way Ibn Kammūna manages to finesse delicate issues, all the while getting across the main points he wishes to make. The deity is introduced thrice. The first time is as the being who brings this world into existence. Ibn Kammūna is careful not to describe Him here as Creator (*muḥdith* or *mubdiʿ* in Arabic), though epithets referring to creation are used towards the end of this first section. The phrase he uses, *mukhrij ilā al-wujūd,* could be taken to mean the one who bestows "existence" upon the cosmos, in keeping with the doctrine of the eternalist philosophers who maintain that the cosmos is co-eternal with deity. This meaning would be very apt for the Avicennan philosophy to which Ibn Kammūna subscribed, though not entirely. These philosophers do hold, however, that the cosmos is dependent for its status as "existing" upon the Supreme Being. The deity is ontologically prior but not temporally so. Ibn Kammūna's formulation accommodates both the creationist and eternalist viewpoints.

The second introduction calls the deity *wājib al-wujūb.* As I have already noted, this is a very widespread designation, and one whose usage moved beyond the confines of the community of philosophers. It is a philosophical appellation that stirs up no antagonism from traditional quarters.

The precise meaning of this appellation, however, is not such a simple matter, and it has been debated in the scholarly literature.

In Arabic, *al-wājib al-wujūd li-dhātihi* is a common philosophical moniker for the deity; though it was not invented by Ibn Sīnā (Avicenna), it appears to be the case that its widespread usage is due in large part to his writings. The phrase aims to express the idea that the deity is not contingent upon anything.[7] Pressing the strict philosophical definition of the phrase might lead to the conclusion that other entities—for example time—are noncontingent. However, it was generally agreed that there could be only one such entity, and that the entity that met the ontological demands of necessary existence was totally identical to and indistinguishable from the entity that governs the cosmos in a free, wise, and unrestricted manner. This entity is also called the "Being who brings this world into existence"—that is to say, confers from its own free and unlimited existence a lesser mode of reality on to this world of ours. Eventually, Ibn Kammūna will demonstrate that this entity is the deity recognized by the faith communities.

Finally, and only on the third time around, Ibn Kammūna refers to Him as the deity (*al-ilāh*), High and Mighty. He takes care to use the noun *ilāh,* rather than the proper name Allāh, even though the latter is perfectly acceptable to Jews and Christians as well as to Muslims.

There are numerous ways to verify these claims about the Supreme Being. However, the most evident path and the one easiest to understand is, to give it its contemporary moniker, the argument from design. Contemplation of the mineral, vegetable, and animal components of our world, as well as of the wondrous arrangements in the heavens, cannot but lead us to the conclusion that they have been made by a wise Governor, one who is also cognizant of what is best for the cosmos and designs everything with the appropriate *telē* (ends) in mind. Ibn Kammūna expressly rejects the model of the "blind watchmaker"; in his words, a well-written document, beautiful both in its calligraphy and the discourse that it conveys, cannot possibly be the result of "the chance flow of ink along the paper."

The proof that a Supreme Being stands at the head of the causal chain that brought about this orderly, teleologically functioning universe derives from the law that every cause must be accompanied by an effect. But the universe could not have come into being—again, this does not necessarily mean the same thing as being created in time—unless an entity existed that has no need of a cause; one that exists for its own sake, a being self-sufficient ontologically, a being that does not need to receive its "existence" from anything else. This being is the deity.

This sort of argument is very widespread in medieval philosophy. However, Ibn Kammūna—following Ibn Sīnā—gives it a twist. He does not include as part of his argument the assertion that the causal chain cannot be infinite; hence it must end at a first cause. Instead, he says that whether the intermediate causes are finite or infinite, there must in either case be an uncaused being, necessary in its own right.

This proof basically argues that every effect, every event or object, must have a cause; if its immediate cause is not a necessity in and of itself—in other words, if it is contingent—it necessarily relies on some other cause. We continue this line of reasoning until we reach a highest cause, one which does not depend upon anything other than itself for its existence. Most proofs of the sort Ibn Kammūna sets down here aim to show that since an infinite regress is impossible, the chain of causation must end at a first, uncaused cause. However, Ibn Kammūna prefers here a different approach, one which allows an infinite number of intermediate causes.[8]

Near the end of this discussion, Ibn Kammūna mentions "the complete cause." Theologians—Shi'ites in particular—distinguished between *al-'illa al-tāmma,* "the complete cause," and *al-'illa al-nāqiṣa,* "the defective [incomplete] cause." The former denotes the cause which is necessary and sufficient for the effect's coming about or, as they would put it, for the effect's existence. The effect needs no other cause for it to be. The defective cause, then, is incomplete; it is necessary but not sufficient for the effect's existence. Put differently, a defective causal chain allows for some contingency; it allows for some freedom of action on the part of a human agent. These concepts find their place in the involved, some might say tortuous, efforts of theologians to maintain both divine decree and human freedom. Thus, for example, some claimed that two angels inscribed the embryo's fate on two different tablets, the one containing complete causes—and hence immutable—and the other with a defective causal chain, leaving room for some human freedom. Here I understand Ibn Kammūna to be arguing that every part, or each particular concatenation of causes needed to produce a specific effect, must exist together; then the effect or event can come about. However, every link within the entire chain, tracing back to the first (divine) cause, need not necessarily exist simultaneously. Once an effect has given way to some other, the cause of the first need not be present. This is similar to Ibn Sīnā's way of allowing an unlimited causal chain.[9]

A possible implication of this position, which I will here only mention in passing, is that Ibn Kammūna does not endorse creation in time if this concept is taken to mean a singular starting point for the material universe's coming into being. (In Chapter Three he will insist that God's knowledge accompanies events as they occur, each at its own moment.) His arguments all turn on the ontological priority of the Necessary Existent, and its bestowing of "existence" down the causal chain.

The chapter ends with another characteristic move on Ibn Kammūna's part: an analogy between the causal chain in Reality and the chain of items acquired in our search for knowledge. The latter begins with immediate (*badīḥī*) knowledge that does not need to undergo the process of acquisition. So also Reality begins with "that which bestows existence" (*al-mūjid*), the being necessary in its own right, which does not need to receive existence from any cause above it. That being is the deity.

Ibn Kammūna draws here an interesting—and perhaps daring—analogy between the relationship of the Necessary Existent to all other existents (subsequent to it ontologically if not temporally) and the relationship of immediate—that is, self-evident—axioms and all other items of knowledge that an individual may acquire. Later on, he will draw an analogy between the immediate, unshakable self-knowledge of the human individual and the self-knowledge of the deity.

The third chapter takes up attributes (properties, descriptions) of the deity that must be confirmed, and another set that must be denied. This was a touchy and controversial topic. On the one hand, it seems necessary to posit certain features that characterize the deity, such as knowledge or immutability. But might not God's knowledge (to give one example) take on an existence of its own, becoming a divine entity that is not totally identical to God Himself? In that case, the cardinal belief in a single god looks to be violated.

In reading this chapter, we must pay careful attention to the order of presentation. One "established fact" entails another; but the chain as it appears in this chapter is not the same as the one Ibn Kammūna describes elsewhere. Here God's knowledge of His creation is the starting point, perhaps because this is the facet closest to the heart of the simpler type of person who is Ibn Kammūna's audience. God's knowledge of His creatures necessarily indicates His knowledge of His own self. How does that work? It must be that the "productive knowledge" of creatures (both things and events) unfolds out of the deity's knowledge of His own essence. The paragraph ends with a citation from the Qur'an, "He is the First and the Last, the Apparent and the Hidden." This verse, which has nearly identical analogues in both the Hebrew Bible and the New Testament, was chosen deliberately for that very reason, as I explained in the preface. "First and Last" refer to God's timelessness; "Apparent and Hidden," if I understand correctly, convey the visible or apparent products of the hidden god.

This last point should be elaborated. The Necessary Being—the God of the philosophers, if you wish—must be sempiternal, without a beginning in time. Events and entities that participate in the temporal flow require a *mūjid,* "that which confers existence." All such events and entities are contingent, containing *ab initio* aspects of existence and nonexistence. It is the *mūjid* which conveys existence by tilting the balance in favor of, or preponderating, existence over nonexistence in each particular event. Were nonexistence a possibility for the Necessary, something would be required to mandate its existence, and its dependence on that something would make it contingent rather than noncontingent and necessary in its own right. Hence the Necessary always has been and always will be. Though it connects to the temporal world by conferring or removing existence in "real time," to use a contemporary and here relevant phrase, in its own sublime existence it is "above time."

The next step is to show that the deity must be simple. The proof runs like this. Knowledge of a compound must be preceded by knowledge of its components or parts. But were God to know one of His parts, and also know that it is He who knows that it is one of His parts, He would then know his own (complete) essence. This leads to a contradiction: He must know His whole both before and after knowing His part. Elsewhere Ibn Kammūna uses an argument of this sort to show that any self-cognizant entity must be simple, the self-cognizant entities being the human soul and the deity. (The angels or immaterial intellects may also be included, but Ibn Kammūna here stresses the analogy between the human soul and the deity.)

In making this argument Ibn Kammūna looks to depart from Avicenna on the question of whether there are any simple bodies. Ibn Kammūna denies that such things exist. Avicenna for his part acknowledged the existence of simple bodies in at least some of his works.[10] (Ibn Kammūna introduces atoms in the next paragraph only for the sake of argument. He surely denies their existence in reality.)

God's knowledge (I will for convenience and smoother English occasionally use *God* instead of the *Necessary* and other epithets) is productive; His knowledge causes events in real time. Hence God's immutability does not entail His ignorance, nor do the dynamics of the universe mandate that an immutable being be ignorant of the events as they happen. God knows and causes events simultaneously, bestowing upon them "existence" out of His boundless sempiternity.

From here Ibn Kammūna proceeds to deny of the deity two characteristics: He is not a body and therefore He is not confined to any place. Though Ibn Kammūna does not propound a strictly negative theology—one in which we can only say what God is not—negations such as these are important. In sum, the "true and holy reality" of God has no equivalent.

This last point is elaborated in two substantial refutations that follow: one rejecting the possibility of two "necessaries," the other arguing, in less abstract terms, that the deity has neither a consort nor a child. The first of these is a foretaste of the following chapter, whose topic is the refutation of dualism. Ibn Kammūna's preoccupation with that competitor to monotheism is somewhat of a mystery. I can detect no clue in his exposition as to a specific sect, religion, or philosophy that he has in mind, or why dualism loomed so large on his theological horizon.

To be sure, the refutation of dualism was a fixture of Islamic philosophical and theological writing; the tenth-century philosopher al-Fārābī, to give just one example, paid it some attention.[11] However, Ibn Kammūna reveals a deeper concern, which should have an explanation in his historical context. One possibility is the role of dualism in anti-Ismaili polemics. The Mongols crushed the Shi'ite Ismaili sect in Iran, and Naṣīr al-Dīn al-Ṭūsī—himself once attracted to Ismaili esotericism—played an important role in negotiating the surrender of the Ismaili fortress at Alamut. A possible explanation for Ibn Kammūna's concern to refute dualism is the role that heresy played in internal Islamic anti-Ismaili polemics. Al-Ghazālī misrepresents (perhaps intentionally) *al-Sābiq* ("the one preceding," or Intellect) and *al-Tālī* ("the one following," or Soul), two important elements in Ismaili cosmology, as two "eternal divinities" (*ilāhān qadimatān*).[12] Ibn Kammūna looked up to al-Ṭūsī, who was both the towering intellectual figure of his generation and someone with close connections to the Mongol court. The refutations of dualism in the *Kalimāt* may have some tie to this episode in sectarian polemics.

The second polemic is surely directed largely at Christianity. Though the rejection of a "female companion" has some other explanation, the deity's begetting a child is certainly to be identified as a Christian belief. Ibn Kammūna's Abrahamic philosophical monotheism, as I call it, has a clear bias in favor of Judeo-Muslim, rather than Judeo-Christian, ideology.

Chapter Three ends with a discussion of the deity's self-contemplation. "Every perfect thing is an object of desire"; since the deity is most perfect, He is His own object of desire. We humans can know that the deity is far more perfect than we are; but the true nature of the excess of His perfection over ours is beyond comprehension. He, the Necessary, the deity, is the most noble perceiver, perceiving the most noble percept with a perception that is most complete. All higher beings—angels and/or unattached intellects, and humans who realize their humanity as well—can take delight in self-contemplation, since their true selves, their true beings, consist in their percepts, their acquired knowledge. In this regard, clearly, the deity is the most honorable being, since in His self-contemplation He contemplates full and complete perfection. Ibn Kammūna asks rhetorically, "How indeed can one draw an analogy between the finite and the infinite?"

Chapter Four, as noted, intends to demonstrate that the "Governor of the Cosmos"—the *kosmokratōr* of the Greeks (and of the pre-Islamic midrash)—has no partner. As I have already observed, the effort that Ibn Kammūna invests in refuting dualism (the notion of two deities jointly responsible for bringing the cosmos into being and managing it) is a puzzle. Perhaps Ibn Kammūna had some reason to believe that his patron would encounter competitive versions of this heresy in Isfahan. In any event, the proofs that Ibn Kammūna musters are interesting, especially the first one, which infers divine unity from human self-perception.

The epistemological primacy of human self-perception, or self-awareness, is one of the outstanding contributions of Ibn Sīnā. *Mutatis mutandis*—and a great deal of mutation is called for—the idea is close to Descartes's "cogito, ergo sum"; but instead of *cogito*, here the initial statement is "I am aware of my own existence." From this all additional knowledge proceeds, and to it everything ultimately returns for its confirmation. Simply put, only one being, when engaged in this self-reflection, can, in encountering its own self, encounter the supremely perfect. Were two such beings possible, they would perforce form a species; and hence each would have a distinguishing mark that set it off from the other. But then neither would be simple; hence neither would be the one and only deity.

Following the lead of Ibn Sīnā, as established in his famous "flying man" thought experiment, Ibn Kammūna makes self-perception or self-awareness the basis of his entire epistemology. In this thought experiment, we are asked to imagine ourselves flying or floating through the air, without any sensory input at all. Yet we would still be aware of our own selves, and of our existence. This means that we have an internal self-awareness that is not dependent on the external world. The first and in many ways the most perceptive and profound study of this turn in medieval philosophy was published by Shlomo Pines over half a century ago. The more recent assessment of Ibn Sīnā's position by Jari Kaukua is "diametrically opposed" to that of Pines.[13] Kaukua, however, generously recognizes the pioneering nature of Pines's study, as well as the fact that some key sources were as yet unavailable in 1954.[14] Ibn Kammūna remarks that the human self, like the divine self, is engaged in uninterrupted self-perception. In a bold and outstanding move, Ibn Kammūna draws a nearly perfect analogy between the human's self-perception and divine self-perception. Perceiving beings differ one from the other in what they perceive in the act of self-perception; those beings that are more perfect, perceive a more perfect being. The "god of the philosophers" is famously thought to do nothing other than contemplate Himself. In His self-perception, He must perceive the most perfect being of all; and, as Ibn Kammūna will argue, only one being can perceive in itself the most perfect being of all.

A second proof is based on the unity of the cosmos. That unity is certainly nothing like the simple, irreducible unity of the deity, but a unity nonetheless on account of the strong interdependence of its parts. Indeed, the entire universe functions as a single organism, for which reason some true philosophers have dubbed it a macro-anthropos (*insān kabīr*).[15] Interconnections of such intensity can be managed or governed by only one single being.

The chapter ends with a very brief rebuttal of the possibility that there be more than one cosmos—which would clearly open the doors for a different Necessary to govern it. This is as close as we come in this cultural context to the debate over multiple universes that we find in medieval European thought. Interestingly enough, Ibn Kammūna does not take a stance on the question of multiple universes. From his point of view, suffice it to say that were the Necessary Being's wisdom to deem it correct to produce another world, another world would be produced, and that world too would reflect the wisdom of the Necessary Being.

Before I move on to Chapter Five, a brief note on Arabic vocabulary and its translation is called for here. *Nafs* in Arabic has two meanings (at least), or, better put, two usages, that are directly relevant to Ibn Kammūna's discussion. *Nafs* means "soul," the homonym of the Hebrew *nefesh,* and the common translation for the Greek *psychē.* However, it is also used as the reflexive pronoun; Greek uses for this forms of *autos.* So, to get directly to the issue, the Delphic maxim, in Greek *gnōthi seauton,* would necessarily in Arabic have the double entendre of "know thyself" and "know thy soul."

The Arabic word *nafs* poses a knotty problem for those working in Avicennan and post-Avicennan philosophy in particular, because of the centrality of self-knowledge or self-awareness in those developments. Perhaps it is in the interest of sharpness and clarity that Ibn Kammūna, at the beginning of Chapter Four, uses the Arabic *dhāt* to refer to the self; in philosophy *dhāt* usually means "essence."[16] Perhaps he does not want to get mired, at this stage (before he takes up the soul in great detail in Part II), in the distinction or lack thereof between the "real person," "the true core identity of the individual," and the soul, with its myriad functions, not all of which are indubitably bound up with the true self.

However, one should not lose sight of the possibilities inherent in the double entendre, and in the stark identification of the self with the soul—an identification that, in my understanding, Ibn Kammūna and his colleagues would enthusiastically sign on to. The self is entirely the same entity as the immaterial, timeless, near-divine entity that is embedded in the body during the human lifespan.

The short fifth and final chapter of the first section deals briefly with two philosophical issues that have great religious import. In philosophical terms, the first topic is the process of emanation of increasingly degraded beings from the Necessary; the least degraded, being imperfect only insofar as their existence is contingent, are nearest to the top of the scheme. The second topic concerns the management of the affairs of this world, which is solely for the good. However, what may be good for the world at large may incidentally not be good for certain individuals. In religious terms, the issues can be named more succinctly: the first is the existence of angels, the second is theodicy.

There does seem to be an odd leap in Ibn Kammūna's exposition. The first two paragraphs in the chapter talk about the "the first caused being." Nothing can be nobler than it because it emanates from the "aspect" of "unicity" (*waḥdāniyya,* "oneness") of the Necessary. In other words, only one small step separates it from the Necessary; its issuing forth from the Necessary makes it "caused"—that is to say, it makes its existence contingent upon the existence of the Necessary. There is only one such entity.

This first created entity goes by a number of names in different languages; it may be identified (though not necessarily so) with the Logos, the Agent Intellect, al-Ghazālī's "obeyed one" (*al-muṭā'*); all function as "chief angels" in whose trust the deity has placed the day-to-day management of the cosmos.[17] However, Ibn Kammūna does not have any particular use for this being, other than as occupying a needed stage in the descent towards the beings (in the plural) that interest him: the angels and, even more, human souls. Angels are needed so as to fill in the gap, so to speak, between the first created being and human souls: "multiplicity will emanate only through intermediaries." Otherwise they are of no interest. However, Ibn Kammūna intimates that some human souls can belong to their higher rank of existence.

Quite deliberately, as it seems, Ibn Kammūna employs religious language in this section of the chapter. He uses a Qur'anic phrase to describe the angels: *al-muqarrabīn*, "those brought close." Human souls that are "prepared" to acquire the necessary (redeeming) knowledge directly in their initial disposition (*fiṭra*) belong to the world "of the angels and the angels that have been brought close."

The First Gate, on Establishing the Governor of the World, He Whose Existence Is Necessary, and His Unicity, as well as Explicating All of the Attributes of His Majesty, and His Providence

Chapter One

Preface

It has been shown in the sapiential sciences that the human soul possesses two faculties, a speculative one and a practical one. The realization of the speculative one consists of knowledge, while the realization of the practical one consists of action. The sciences and the practices are many and ramified, to the extent that it is beyond human capacity to completely master one of them, let alone all of them. The ancients have settled upon the classification of knowledge, its division into sections, and its further division into parts, as well as clarifying its paths and making clear its gateways. They acted in a similar fashion with regard to the varieties of proper conduct (*adab*) and the sorts of ethical [rules] (*akhlāq*) and political philosophies (*siyāsāt*). Whoever wishes to apprise himself of all of this must study their books carefully, those who lived earlier and those who lived later. Generally speaking, they did not leave anything for anyone after them to say, nor did they leave room for anything to be added.

Now some say that they did not state the finer points with precision. This may be deduced [142] from the fact that they laid down principles for us, in which regard they did not leave out anything that appertains to this world or the next. They rather made a clear statement about them and opened the gates of knowing for them. Given that there is no way to encompass all that has been said about items of knowledge and practice, it is incumbent upon the seeker of perfection to focus his attention upon that which is the best and most important concerning his religion and this-worldly life.

The masters of traditional religions as well as [the masters] of intellectual tenets agree that salvation and eternal felicity depend upon belief in God, [belief in] the end of days, and doing good works. He [the seeker] will then progress in this science to the attributes of God Most High, stripping away [material attributes], and making Him one; clarifying His existence and His providence; and knowing the human soul and her endurance after the destruction of the body, her everlastingness, purification, and the circumstance of her afterlife and second emergence; and [knowing] what is the cause that necessarily brings about her perfection and bliss, as well as that which entails her sinning and failure (*khidhlān*).

The intelligent person (*ʿāqil*) must exert himself to know all of this. For were he to put the lie to the people of wisdom and revelation without backing this up with proof and evidence, he would not be counted among the people of intelligence, revelation, and accomplishment. But were he to believe in that which they agree upon and take it to be true—and that is what is incumbent on him—then the necessity for him to exert himself towards [the acquisition of] this knowledge is plain to see. Furthermore, should he, being in doubt about their teaching, waver between affirming and denying before he may establish that the truth is to affirm them, in that case exertion of this sort would be most prudent for him. Moreover, were a person wary of taking the road upon which there is a preying lion, even though he doubts the truthfulness of the person who reported it, in that case reason mandates that he not take that road out of caution. There is no harm in this, even if there were no lion there.

You must know that knowledge is the pole upon which [everything] turns. It is the root to which one adheres, while practice is the branch that follows upon it. That which most people devote themselves to, calling it knowledge, is not knowledge of the true reality (*ḥaqīqa*). Instead, true knowledge, which ensues after [acquiring the knowledge] described above, consists in that which increases the insight of the servant into his own shortcoming, as well as his knowledge about the worship of [143] his Lord. He should lessen his longing for this world and increase his longing for the next world.

This [holds true] as well when he [the aspirant] does not orient himself in the direction of God Most High and does not have this in mind when he studies. Even though his soul is healthy, he is yet in the true nature of his study involved in the sciences of this world, not the sciences of the next world. True knowledge means that [knowledge] by way of which one turns one's countenance towards the highest refuge (*janāb*) and the holy presence. Whosoever should, by its [knowledge's] means, deviate from that direction, descending so as to acquire by its means some of the rubble of this world and to become closer thereby to its denizens, is intent on error and has joined the troop of fools and ignoramuses. We put our trust in God that our speech not be different from our action, and that our outward behavior not be at variance with our innermost self.

Knowledge of the true reality is a wide ocean and a distant road. Whoever does not penetrate deeply into the seas of its details and does not advance along its pathways and straits can do no less than to satisfy himself with that which I have recorded on these pages.

Chapter Two

On establishing the existence of the Governor of the cosmos, He whose existence is necessary for its own sake; and showing that He is powerful, knowing, willful, and wise; and that He [exercises] providential care over His creatures

The first thing required of the seeker after salvation and perfection is to verify for himself the existence of a Being who brings this world into existence. He is the One whose existence is necessary for its own sake, and He is the Deity, High and Mighty.

The ways of verifying this are many and well known. However, the easiest one to take, the one most ready to embark upon, the most completely evident and closest to understanding is the one taken upon reflecting on the ingenuity and precision found in the beings which [make up] the cosmos, the beauty of their composition, which [path] leads to the orderliness which is the intended goal. Just as this [path] indicates the existence of the One who produced [or "chose"], it also points toward His knowledge, power, will, and providence.

[144] When an intelligent person looks closely at writing that has a beautiful form and order, the discourse which is read from it being well arranged, he will have no doubt that it is the work of a talented scribe; it has not come about from the chance flow of ink along the paper, for example. All the more so will this be the case when he contemplates the orbs and their stars, their placements and motions, the magnitudes of their bodies and distances, and their effects on the lower world; the arrangement of the elements and their interactions by means of their forms and qualities; and the attainment of their mixtures, following upon which the mineral, vegetable, and animal compounds come to be. He knows the psychic, celestial, and terrestrial powers and souls, their origins, and special properties; he thinks about their separable limbs, such as bones, cartilage, arteries, and nerves, and the compound ones, like the head, hand, intestine, eyes, and ears; how some of them were made to be leaders, and others to be led; how souls are joined to bodies, their faculties flowing through them; how animals are directed by inspiration towards what is good for them; how tools and limbs have been prepared for them that suit what is embedded in their nature, such as the tools of prey or swimming, or the snout with which the flea has been created: though it is soft, it has

placed within it the strength to plunge into tough flesh in order to suck out the blood which is suited for it; and other wonders and items of wisdom which we have no way of fully enumerating. I do not think that an intelligent person can reflect upon all of this without it leading him to a decisive indication that the Governor knows the order and good that are [intrinsic to external] reality, and that He wills the good and perfection to the fullest possible extent.

Now that this has been established, I say: If this Governor is that whose existence is necessary for its own sake (*wājib al-wujūd li-dhātihi*), then He is the deity (*ilāh*), praised and exalted. If not, it is still not something that cannot exist, since we have assumed that it does exist. Hence, were it not to be necessary, it would be [merely] possible and existing on account of something else; so what we are speaking about reverts to that something else. It must eventually end up at the first [and] necessary [being]; otherwise, every preceding being, which, by supposition, is a possible governor, has yet to come into existence on its own. Then it is judged to be a "middle" [145], whether it be finite or infinite. This is so because each and every one of the effects requires an originator (*mūjid*) who is not one of them; otherwise, it [the originator] would be included in their domain (*ḥukm;* i.e., would itself be an effect rather than a cause or originator of an effect). Now since the [existence of each] preceding [existent] is known from the existence of each [later] one, even if the intermediates are many, then the last of the effects whose existence is known will accordingly prove the existence of the first of the causes. The necessity of the accompaniment by a cause for the necessity of the effect confirms this. It is confirmed (*taḥaqqaqa*) by the necessary accompaniment by a cause in order for the result to be necessary. Indeed, there are no barriers—as far as the intellect is concerned—for created things that precede one another in time to have no limit in sempiternity [an eternity that has no beginning].

This accompaniment (*muṣāḥaba;* i.e., effect accompanying the cause) is proven by [the fact that] there is no meaning to the necessity of an effect through its cause other than its proceeding (*ṣudūr;* here, "following directly upon," hence "accompanying" it) from it; it will not bring it about in a state of its [the effect's] nonbeing. Otherwise it would join its existence and its nonexistence. Therefore, it [the cause] has an effect [only] when it [the effect] exists [literally, "in the state of its existence"]; but in the case of an absence of a cause, the existence of the effect does not emanate [and so there is no effect]. That which bestows existence (*mūjid;* the cause) and that which receives existence (*mūjad;* the effect) accompany each other in existence (*wujūd*).

Hence the complete causes and their effects are present as long as they exist simultaneously. They [the causes] have a "first" which is the Necessary in its own right (*li-dhātihi*).

Thus, just as we would not attain the acquired items of knowledge were it not for knowledge that is immediate (*badīhī*) and does not need to be acquired, so also were it not for the existence of the Necessary which has no need of that which bestows existence, the contingent that requires it [the Necessary] would not exist. Since that which creates a well-ordered (*muḥkam*) effect must have a wider scope of authority than its effect, there must be a terminus for originators whose knowledge is [all-]encompassing, whose power is perfect, and whose authority is of [the widest] scope. It is the deity Most High.

Chapter Three

On clearly establishing a cluster of [attributes] that must be established of the Necessary, and the negation of a cluster [of attributes] that must be denied of Him

The Necessary's knowledge is productive (*fiʿlī*). Changes [all the dynamics in the universe] stem from it, since it [His knowledge] encompasses them, at the times [of their occurrences], in perpetuity. Therefore, He does not change along with the change in the objects of His knowledge. Ignorance [of particular events] and change [in His knowledge as they change] would be necessary consequences [only] if His knowledge were passive, following upon the existence of the [particular earthly event or] thing and its disappearance [146]. The Necessary is necessarily eternal, since each event (*ḥādith*) requires something to give it existence (*mūjid*); and it [the Necessary] demands sempiternity, since, were it possible for it not to exist, it would require a preponderating factor (*rājiḥ*) which would give preponderance to its aspect of existence over its aspect of nonexistence, and it would thus be contingent. "He is the First and the Last, the Apparent and the Hidden" [Qur'an 57:3].

Now that His knowledge of His creations is established, and it necessarily proves His Knowledge of His own Essence [or "self"; *dhāt*], it then must be the case that He is not compound. For knowledge of the compound depends upon knowledge of each one of its parts; thus knowledge of the part is essentially prior to knowledge of the whole. But were the whole [here the All, the Necessary] to know its part, which is other than it, it would [also] know that it is He who knows it, which would mandate its knowing its essence. Then knowledge of the whole would be prior to knowledge of the part. But the matter is contrary to this [having assumed or established that knowledge of the part must precede knowledge of the whole]; and this is impossible.

Now, since He is not compound, He is not a body, because every body is a compound possessing parts (*dhū ab'āḍ*). Moreover, since He is not a body, He is not confined to place (*mutaḥayyaz*), because that which is confined to place and is indivisible is either a point in place (*fī maḥall*) or a separate substance that does not divide in any way, if such a thing may exist. But both of these [options] mandate that that which grants existence to this world be small and paltry in the extreme—God be greatly exalted above this! In order to exist, the point has a special need of something else in order to inhere within it. However, requiring something else in order to exist negates the necessity of [the thing's] existence however you may have it. Thus the Necessary is above inhering in a place.

Moreover, its true and holy reality (*ḥaqīqa*) is not equivalent to the true reality of any of the contingent beings. Otherwise, contingency [or "possibility"] would be mandated, rather than necessity, since similar things must be equivalent in their requisites (*lawāzim*). Were there to come about two individuals in the species of the necessary [i.e., two necessary existents, two Necessaries], each would be distinguished from the other by means of its specification (*ta'yīn*). That which they share is different from their specification; thus the Necessary is compounded of the two of them [shared and specific or non-shared particulars]. But if the specification of each is that it is the Necessary Existent, then there is no Necessary other than it! But if the matter is otherwise [it has a specification other than the necessity of its existence], then with regard to its specification it has some other [exterior] cause [and hence is contingent]. But if it is not caused, then the particularization of each one with regard to its specification is [done] without a particularizer. This is false.

[147] Hence nothing is found to share in His true reality; He has neither a female companion nor a child. How could one represent to oneself something detaching itself from that which is not compound, so that it becomes its equivalent in species or genus, and thus is its child? Were something other than Him from among His creations to be His equivalent in its full true reality, neither one would be more entitled than the other [to be the Necessary], insofar as one is a creator and the other is a creation.

Therefore, the Necessary will not inhere in a place. It has no opposite who either succeeds it in its place or joins together with it in it; nor does it have an opposite in the sense of something that is equal to it in power and can prevent it.

[148] Every perfect thing is an object of desire. Therefore, the Necessary perceives Himself exactly as He is in beauty and clarity. [So also does He perceives that] He is the Origin of all beauty and clarity and the wellspring of all good and order. Hence, among those who take delight in themselves, He is the most honorable, because He is the most noble perceiver of the most noble percept with the most complete perception. His delight in perceiving Himself, relative to our delight in perceiving ourselves, is analogous to His perfection relative our perfection. But only He perceives His perfection just as He is. We are not capable of understanding any of the characteristics of the Necessary for its own sake unless it be by analogy to what we know about ourselves [our souls]. Still we know that they [the true characteristics of the Necessary] are more perfect, more noble, and more sublime than whatever it is that we understand concerning our own true

selves (*ḥaqq anfasunā*). But we do not know the true nature of that excess [of the Necessary over ourselves], since nothing like it is found in our portion. How indeed can one draw an analogy between the finite and the infinite? [It cannot be done], neither in [their relative] intensity nor in their quantity. No characteristic of the First Necessary has its match among us; hence we have no way of comprehending Him. We will only take note of that which lies within our knowing it—not that we have any claim to it in its essence.

Chapter Four

That the Governor of the Cosmos is one and has no partner

His unicity [oneness] is proven by [the fact that] the human, when he perceives his [own] self (*dhāt*) and points to it [gestures mentally towards his own self] will find in his self only something that perceives itself. Everything else is unknown, be it real or unreal [something that exists or something whose existence is denied]: it is exterior to his self. He does not perceive his self by means of a form that is added to his self [i.e., the percept is not a "form" added to the self; it is rather the very self]. Indeed, every form that is added onto the self is indicated from its [the self's] direction; and it [the self] indicates its own self by means of "I." Its perception cannot be dissevered from its self. The realities susceptible to perception (*al-ḥaqā'iq al-idrākiyya*) differ only with regard to perfection or shortcoming, and in external matters.

Now that this has been established [we proceed]: were it true that there are two Necessaries, each one of them perceiving its own self, [149] its [each one's] perception of its own self would not add anything to its own self. Now if one differs from the other with regard to perfection or shortcoming, then the perfect one is the deity, rather than the one that falls short. But if they are equivalent in this regard, then the two of them belong to a species. In that case, one of them must be distinguished from the other, beyond its sharing with it the reality susceptible to perception, by means of something. Therefore, it is compound, and hence it is not a deity.

That it is impossible for there to be two deities for this world is proven also from the intensity of the bonding of its [the world's] parts, one to the other. For example, accidents cannot do without their substances in one contemplation, and, in another contemplation, substances [are in need of] their accidents. So also its [the world's] things that are confined to place, its abstract items, its elemental and celestial [parts], its animals, plants, and its simple and compound things. Likewise, some animals are in need of others, and the organs of a single individual are in need of each other; its humors and spirits [also stand in need of] each other. Indeed, the parts of the cosmos support one another to such an extent that it is like one compound individual. For this reason, some of those who speak the truth (*al-muḥaqqaqin;* "verifiers") dub it a macroanthropos (*insān kabīr*).

Thus, should one of the two deities act independently in his governance, the other would have no effect in it; otherwise, two effectuators would join together in [producing] a single effect, and one of them would be unnecessary. But were he to act independently only in part of it [the desired effect], while the other [acts independently] in the other part, there would be no connection or cooperation between the two parts.

Next: [when] one is an agent [of some entity or event], and then another entity follows upon its [the first event's] existence, and [that same] other benefits from it [the first event], in that case, only one of the two is responsible for bringing into being the two things or in governing them, and no more need be said (*fa-ḥasbu*). The impossibility of one of them acting independently in governing everything for one period of time and the other's governing it for some other period of time is obvious to the folk of true realities (*ahl al-ḥaqā'iq*).

Were it possible for another world to exist, having no connection to this world, then the goodness, mercy, and unlimited power of the Necessary would mandate its being brought into being. His perfection, which knows no limit, mandates that none of the contingent beings, or any aspect of good order and governance, be left behind. Rather, it would issue forth from His holy essence, and it would require as well His providence and far-reaching wisdom.

Chapter Five

On how the Governing Necessary [Being] acts; the emanation of the contingent beings from Him; and establishing the existence of the angels

A baser contingent being can exist only if a nobler contingent being has existed before it. Nothing more excellent than the first caused being may exist because the Necessary Being has mandated it from the aspect of His unicity. There remains no aspect that would mandate something more noble than it. Were one to suppose an entity more noble than it, this would call for an aspect that is more noble than that obtaining for the Necessary Being, and that is absurd.

Were two things to emanate from a single aspect of the True One (*al-wāḥid al-ḥaqīqiyy*), they would differ from one another by means of some criterion; otherwise, they would not be two [different] things. The relation (*nisba*) of the caused beings to the confines of existence (*muqayyad al-wujūd*) would then be equivalent, no one of them having something that the other lacks; then that which is more than one would be one, and this is obviously false.

For this reason, the existence of angels brought close, which some call intellects, is manifest. Were there not to exist contingent beings that are more noble than immaterial (*mujarrada*) souls, the souls would not exist at all, in line with the principle that you already know: from that which is one from every aspect, multiplicity will emanate only through intermediaries. The goodness of the Creator will not allow any neglect in bringing into existence a parcel and portion of knowledge (*ma'rifa;* gnosis) for everyone who has prepared himself [for it]. If this preparation is in the initial, innate disposition (*awwal al-fiṭra*), without any intermediary, then it belongs to the world of angels that have been brought close. If it has reached an impasse (*tawaqqafa;* "stopped") in acquiring through the intermediary of those who have been brought close or something else [which can function as an intermediary in the transmission of knowledge] that [knowledge] which is not mandated, then it is the world of the celestial angels; they are the celestial souls. After them follow the ranks of the rest of the souls.

There is no good thing with reference to contingency but that the Creator's (*al-khāliq*) knowledge is bound to it, and His might and goodness mandate its coming into being. There is no bad thing with reference to contingency but that His knowledge is bound to it, and His mercy mandates that it be repelled. However, the good is mandated essentially, whereas the bad is mandated accidentally. The Creator (*al-bāri'*) will not leave aside something that has a great deal of good on account of a little bit of bad that it contains, because leaving it aside would annihilate the great deal of good. He does not [151] seek to hand out the good thing in order to be perfected by it [by this good act]; instead, handing out the good to the other belongs to His perfection. Indeed, seeking the good and wishing for it is more suitable for Him, just as existence is more suitable for reality than its nonexistence.

None of this, however, entails His being perfect on account of something else. That would be the case only if the will and the thing willed—each one of them—were more suitable for Him. But since it is only the will to bring benefit to the other that is more suitable, without His attaining perfection by means of the thing willed upon, then it is not so.

This is what the occasion requires of me to mention in connection with the circumstances of the Origin. I shall now follow up on this with the circumstances of the hereafter (*al-ma'ād*), with the help of God and His good granting of success.

PART I.
ON KNOWLEDGE
SECOND GATE

Synopsis and Commentary

Throughout his career Ibn Kammūna maintained a special interest in the "science of the soul"; his exertions to verify the soul's immortality in particular border on an obsession. In most of his philosophical writings Ibn Kammūna serves up a variety of proofs for the soul's immortality, often coming up with new and different arguments. He penned several monographs whose main goal was to demonstrate the soul's permanent endurance.[1] It comes as no surprise, then, that half of the section in this treatise, or one-quarter of the *Kalimāt*, is dedicated to *'ilm*, knowledge or science, and deals with knowledge of the soul.

The first chapter opens with one of the definitions of the soul that became very popular in the Avicennan tradition. The soul is the referent of *I* whenever someone states something in the first person, e.g., "I did such and such." All of the bodily faculties are under the soul's control and act as her agents. Although some theorists may place biological systems under the control of different "souls," all of these souls are nonetheless subservient to the one chief soul, the referent of *I*.

Perception, emotion, and other capacities of the soul all derive from one single soul, which is the identical referent of both *I*s in a sentence such as "I sensed and so I became irritated." This same point (and the same example) is made by Ibn Sīnā, who writes: "We say, 'when I perceived such and such a thing, I became angry.' . . . So it is one and the same thing which perceives and becomes angry."[2]

Several different theories of the soul, or souls, that superintend the human organism as well as attending to emotions, ratiocination, and more, were in circulation. Ibn Kammūna briefly alerts the reader to the possibilities, without citing any sources by name. Plato introduced a tripartite theory of the soul in his *Republic*, book 4, and his theory was developed and forcefully advocated by Galen.[3] The Platonic-Galenic tradition spoke of three "souls," each located in one of the three chief organs: the liver, the heart, and the brain. Ibn Kammūna can live with that theory, so long as it is agreed that one soul has the role of commander-in-chief. Indeed, the Galenic tradition does recognize a hegemonikon. In his arguments against transmigration, Ibn Sīnā negated the view that two souls, one rational and the other animal, could inhabit the same body.[4] Perhaps it was with that in mind that Ibn Kammūna adds that two chief souls cannot be responsible for one body.

Another theory held that the soul is an expression of the congruous composition or "harmony" of the material constituents of the body. Ibn Kammūna penned a special monograph in order to refute that doctrine, which he found to be noxious because it contradicted his views on the eternity of the soul both before and after its temporal residence in the human organism.[5]

Ibn Kammūna is especially concerned with the stability of the individual's identity (or, perhaps, self-identification) over the course of a lifetime of changes. As we shall see, he hedges on the question of transmigration (or, more accurately, metensomatosis); if the same soul resides in different human bodies over the course of time, the question of identity becomes more acute. Identity is very much a modern issue, though traces of the notion can be found in antiquity and the medieval period.[6] For Ibn Kammūna, the fixed identity to which *I* refers whenever I speak of myself is critical. Personal improvement, through ethical refinement and the acquisition of knowledge, is indeed pivotal for the way of life he advocates. These changes all affect the same immortal, immaterial core person; if we cannot speak of transforming this core person (Ibn Kammūna is reticent on the subject), nonetheless the constellation of characteristics that are acquired in a lifetime are deeply enough assimilated to survive the death of the body and reemerge in a new life.

The soul can never be unaware of herself. True, the temporal human instantiation may be unaware of the soul that it bears, but the soul's very existence is intimately bound with her self-awareness. Nonetheless, the soul is perforce unaware of every bodily organ at some moment. Hence—if I follow Ibn Kammūna here—the soul cannot be identified with any bodily organ, for that would be mean that, for at least one moment, the soul was both aware and unaware of herself.

Chapter Three deals with the indestructibility of the soul. The issue is clearly of great importance, and Ibn Kammūna musters several proofs. To begin with, he argues that the soul is not complex; it is not something that passes from potentiality to actuality, and then back again. Clearly, then, complexities or compounds are not indestructible. However, there is a crucial difference between a compound, which exists so long as the bonds holding its parts together are *in actu,* and an indestructible essence that is at times manifest and at others not, depending on that essence's relationship to some material organ.

Ibn Kammūna illustrates this point by means of vision, an essence for the sake of this argument, and the eye. As an essence, vision is always *in actu;* but in its connection to the eye, it is a power or faculty that moves back and forth between potentiality and actuality. The faculty of vision has a substratum; it is located within the eye. When the person is asleep, or in a dark place, or dies, vision is only a potentiality in his eye; when he is awake and in the presence of light, it activates. Eternal essences are always active, but their manifestation moves in and out of actuality by virtue of a relationship or connection with a substrate. When that material substrate disintegrates, the potentiality that had inhered in it is lost. The essence, however, lives on. Vision as such, vision as an essence, will never cease to exist. So also the human soul is always *in actu*—she is always aware of herself, even if the person bearing her is not—and hence will never perish; she will never cease to exist.

Yet another argument for the claim that the simplicity of the soul entails her indestructability appeals silently to an idea usually associated with the kalam. Complex things exist by virtue of their complexity; the very fact of the coalescence of the components gives the complex object its existence. By the same token, the disintegration of the compound is enough to make the compound nonexistent, even though its components remain. This is not the case for simple substances, which can only be nullified by "accepting nonexistence." But should an existing entity accept nonexistence, it would, if only momentarily (Ibn Kammūna does not discuss the temporal aspects of this issue here), be characterized by both existence and nonexistence. Since such a situation is impossible, the simple entity (soul, for example) can never not exist.[7]

Some schools of the kalam viewed nonexistence as an accident that attaches to an entity, thus bringing about its nullification.[8] Reversing the order, we find an entity having now the property of nonexistence replacing its accident of nonexistence with the accident of existence, and thus coming to be; but such an entity is not simple. Something complex—either a complex object, such as a compound, or an "inherence" that belongs to a complex material substrate such as the body—must be actualized in order to move from nonexistence to existence. Not so absolutely simple substances, which are also self-standing, meaning that they possess an inherent reality or existence and do not stand in need of any outside source which will bequeath reality upon them, in the way material compounds do. In brief, only things that are complex and not self-standing will come and go out of existence (i.e., actuality). The soul is neither of these, and hence it will always exist.

Towards the end of Chapter Three Ibn Kammūna proceeds to demonstrate the indestructibility of the soul by systematically eliminating all possible causes of a thing's annihilation. These are self-annihilation; something whose presence would prevent it from existing, namely an "opposite" that disables the thing's entry point (*madkhal*) into existence, by occupying that entry point itself; and the absence of that presence is mandatory for its existence—namely, a condition (in the sense of a precondition or restraint required for something to be or to happen).

Reality, or the class of existing things, may be divided into those which require a substrate (*maḥall*) in which they abide and those which do not. A member of the first group may have its abode seized by an opposite, thus denying it an entry point into existence, since only one thing can populate that abode. But the soul (a self-standing substance) requires no abode, hence her entry point into reality cannot be denied. Moreover, there is no precondition for her existence, since the permanence of her cause (the agent responsible for her existence) guarantees her endurance.[9]

In his *New Wisdom,* Ibn Kammūna develops a fuller and more sophisticated doctrine of existence and nonexistence, one that has been studied in detail, especially with reference to its sources, by Heidrun Eichner, who briefly notes the thirteenth-century synthesis between the kalam and Avicennan philosophy with regard to the category of nonbeing.[10] Different proofs refuting the possible nonexistence of the soul are developed at great length in Ibn Kammūna's monograph on the immortality of the soul; the bulk of those arguments are deployed to show that—*pace* Ibn Sīnā—the soul is not incipient, but preexisting before entering the body.[11]

The death of the human individual is defined as the dissevering of the soul from the body. Ibn Kammūna remarks, "The dissolution (*inḥilāl*) is a certain motion that traces back to the heavenly motions, just as it has been determined in the well-known books." Two interesting features of this statement should be noted. First, he calls the dissevering an *inḥilāl,* a word formed from the same root as *ḥulūl,* "inherence." This need not pose a problem; the verb *inḥalla* is very commonly used in the sense of untying a knot. However, near the beginning of this section Ibn Kammūna went to some length to refute the claim that the soul's connection to the body should be described as a *ḥulūl.* He might have wished to use a different word, then, to indicate the soul's disseverance from the body. Second, Ibn Kammūna refers to the "well-known books" on astral governance. In his system, the heavenly bodies play no role in the production of the soul, or in her emanation, since she preexists; nor do the astral bodies belong to the entities possessing per se a higher standing than the human soul. They do play a role in earthly life, though, specifically in being responsible for the ultimate demise of the body, after which the soul can no longer inhabit it.

Ibn Kammūna hints here at his belief that the soul can relocate herself after death in a new and different body. Moreover, it is not just the core soul, but her psychic configuration as well. This configuration is made up of qualities that were acquired or lost in the preceding earthly existence and are not essential to the soul. Ostensibly they should dissipate along with the death of the body, but this is not so, according to Ibn Kammūna. Death is nothing but "a certain motion" directed by the stars which destroys the body but not the link between the soul's agent or cause and her configuration or accidents. The psychic configuration that is basically responsible for the individual personality each one of us has need not come apart when the soul departs the body, and this very same psychic configuration preserves its coherence by means of its relation to its higher, immaterial and immortal cause. It will later settle into a new substratum. This doctrine calls to mind Indian notions of transmigration, where karma but also positive achievements are carried on to the next incarnation, thus affording the individual a better starting point for his new life.[12] The configuration as such, or perhaps one or more of its thoroughly embedded characteristics, may be considered accidents of the soul. We have here a clear statement on the possibility of transmigration. Ibn Kammūna leans toward that doctrine but is careful not to declare outright support for it.

Throughout the *Kalimāt* Ibn Kammūna flirts as it were with the notion of transmigration and the possibility that the soul—not just her essence but also the configuration of properties she has acquired and made her own in the course of a lifetime—can be instantiated in another body. Perhaps—again, Ibn Kammūna seems to be deliberately discreet when talking about this—this new instantiation allows the soul to pick up where she left off in her previous bodily sojourn and progress further. However, when she is finally disembodied without any further attachment to human bodies—a sort of nirvana—then her self-awareness, and her perception of intelligibles, is most complete and perfect.

Ibn Kammūna takes great strides in order to consolidate this point, perhaps even proposing a new physics of accidents, so as to allow them to maintain their configuration in the process of transmigration. It is not entirely clear whether Ibn Kammūna has in mind a series of transmigrations or the final resurrection that is agreed upon by all that he notes in the introduction, but the point is not critical for his argument here. According to him, the constellation of characteristics does not undergo local motion or anything similar in the process of transmigration. Rather, its supernal cause has them manifest themselves in one abode and then in another. The psychic configuration manifests itself in its human residence the way an image manifests itself in a mirror. The analogy to a mirror is found in the Persian mystical poetry of Jalāl al-Dīn Rūmī, where Husam is the spiritual mirror image of Shams.[13] This is one passage in the *Kalimāt* where a Buddhist influence, drawn specifically from the *Abhidharma-Kośa-śāstra* of Vasubandhu, seems to be most evident.[14]

Near the end of the fourth chapter in this section, Ibn Kammūna makes an even stronger statement: the psychic configuration acquired in the course of a lifetime can be removed from the soul upon the death of the body only by some "removing agent"—but there is no proof that such a "removing agent" exists. To sum up: none of the possibilities for nonexistence or annihilation obtain for the soul; hence she is indestructible.

The most significant divergence of Ibn Kammūna from the Avicennan legacy is the former's endorsement of the soul's preexistence: that is, its existence in eternity before entering into the body. Clearly, this stance is related to his firm defense of the soul's permanence; for Ibn Kammūna the soul is a substance to which "nonexistence" has never and will never be affiliated.

However, the permanence of the soul, and the related idea of the stability of a person's identity, are not above challenging. They may be self-evident to Ibn Kammūna, in the simplistic sense that the soul's stability is evident to herself. She knows that she is the same entity that she had been years ago, despite all that she has gone through in the intervening years. However, the stability of the self (*nafs* can mean both "soul" and "self"; *dhāt* means "self" as well as "essence" and related concepts; it is not clear to me just how strictly Ibn Kammūna differentiates between the terms) should require further examination. Modern philosophers as far back as David Hume and most forcefully in our own day Derek Parfit have cast into doubt the very notion of a stable self. Indeed, Buddhists (though not all schools of Buddhism) had long ago denied the existence of the stable self, and it is very likely that Ibn Kammūna was exposed to Buddhist thought by way of his connections with the Mongol court. Clearly, however, Buddhist denial of the self had no impact on Ibn Kammūna, even as a theory that must be refuted.

From the theoretical perspective, Ibn Kammūna does not speak much about the changing, developing, or evolving self. He does not move beyond the teachings of Ibn Sīnā and al-Suhrawardī, his two principal sources in psychology, with regard to the stable self. However, from the standpoint of ethics, real, substantive change is imperative; and half of the *Kalimāt* is devoted to the practices which, in one way or another, aim at the perfection of the self.

The final paragraph in Chapter Two reads almost like a fallback position. Whether or not the soul is taken to be immaterial, she must be the ultimate authority of the person's actions. It is to the soul that one traces back all actions; the soul is not the agent of any higher authority within the person.

As I have already noted, in the third chapter Ibn Kammūna returns to the permanence or immortality of the soul—a preoccupation to which he devoted a great deal of his energies and manifested the originality of his contributions. I have already called attention to the claim that the indestructibility of the soul is due in large measure to her simplicity. She is not a complex entity that can break up or an inherence whose existence depends upon the thing within which it inheres.

Nonetheless, the soul and other immaterial simples are not uncaused; that would confer upon them the status of the Necessary Existent and lead in effect to a plurality of divinities. Ibn Kammūna is clearly aware that there is a real or at the very least apparent contradiction between the soul's essential simplicity, which is a necessary feature of the supernal, sublime status that he wishes to confer upon her, and the fact that she is caused, indeed, not directly by God but by way of intermediaries; and to be caused is to have some inescapable duality. The full proof for the soul's essential simplicity is subtle and probably not free of casuistry. The interested reader must work his or her way through the translation. Suffice it to note here that Ibn Kammūna is well aware that the simplicity of the soul is no simple matter. Moreover, he is no less aware that the higher types of immaterial beings, which in his reading are the "efficient causes" of human souls, have been recognized in different traditions and given different names: "angels, intellects, or some other name."

How does this help his argument about the permanent endurance of the soul? Quite simply, the soul will exist as long as her causes, both proximate and remote, exist. But the connection here with the "First Necessary"—i.e., God—is different from that of material objects (certainly compound ones). Hence Ibn Kammūna can conclude that in the case of the soul, as well as of the immaterial entities above her in the causal chain, each must exist as long as the "First Necessary" does—which means forever.

A bit later in this same chapter, Ibn Kammūna will discuss the contingency of the human soul, an immaterial substance that has a cause. He will conclude that the human soul could cease to exist only if her ultimate immaterial cause ceased to exist. That ultimate cause is the Necessary Existent (by way of intermediaries, angels or intellects as you may wish to call them), which of course never ceases to exist. Hence the human soul will also never cease to exist.

Ibn Kammūna goes even farther: when the soul's bond with the body is dissolved at death, it is not just the "core" soul which maintains herself. The particular constellation or configuration of accidents which make up the individual's personality can also be preserved, and reinstated, in a new substratum—though Ibn Kammūna, here and throughout his work, is careful not to declare himself openly in support of metensomatosis. Death is interpreted as a "certain motion" and as a lapse in the soul's manifestation in a sensible, material entity. These claims are supported by a series of subtle metaphysical arguments, the gist of which is the continuous, unbroken, and permanent causal connection between the soul and her causes.

At the end of the chapter Ibn Kammūna adds what he calls "an intuitive argument." Anyone perceptive enough to recognize the wisdom of the Creator and His providence over creation will come to the conclusion that man's final purpose cannot be his transient stay on earth. An everlasting felicity is man's ultimate destiny; and because that felicity is so sweet, he fears losing it so much—which, I might add, seems to be an explanation for our mistaken fear of death. This argument may be helpful to someone who cannot himself intuit more rigorous proofs; but in any case, the soul's indestructibility has already been given a "dependable proof" in the preceding.

In the fourth chapter of this section Ibn Kammūna addresses the destiny of the soul and her ultimate perfection. The soul belongs to the class of immaterial beings. These are ranked differently; the closer they are to the "Necessary" (also called in this chapter the "Highest Excellency"), the more its pure light shines upon them, and the more intense their perception of that highest being. The soul's goal is to maximize her proximity (note that Ibn Kammūna does not mention union) to the "Highest Excellency." The proximity of immaterial entities one to the other is measured by the intensity of their perception; clearly a powerful soul will perceive more intensely. According to a widely accepted notion, inherited by Islamicate philosophers from the Hellenes, the First Being engages in a delightful awareness of its own essence; it is delightful because of the sublimity of the divine essence which it contemplates unendingly. By extension, the human soul takes delight in being aware of things, but this delight varies depending on the object of her awareness. No awareness is totally barren, since every essence (*dhāt*) has some shadow at least cast by the light of the First Being. The higher the being in the "great chain," the more it perceives of this first, true light, and the more intense its delight. Clearly, the aim and task of the soul is come as close as possible to the true light of the First Being.

The soul's ranking on this scale has an upper boundary vis-à-vis higher beings, angels, or intellects, but within the segment allotted to human souls there is also a range of locations. The main impediment to the soul's intensifying her perception of the highest being is her necessary preoccupation with the body. Hence during sleep, when the soul need not attend so much to the body, she is especially receptive to revelations in the form of dreams. The soul receives by way of dreams sublime items of knowledge that she cannot receive when in a waking state and occupied with absorbing information by way of the external senses.[15]

Ibn Kammūna also brings into the discussion visions in the waking state, which can overwhelm those whose souls are not powerful enough to withstand them. He thus concludes on a cautionary note: "But for the person whose soul is not strong, that [dream or vision] may lead to his senses being startled and his imagination perturbed; perhaps his senses and imagination were like that in their original makeup. That is a deficiency which is not praiseworthy." It is not quite clear to me just what Ibn Kammūna is getting at here. Is he seeking to have his account encompass those who go nearly mad from a vision, without denying that the vision is a true linking with the "Highest Excellency"? Might this be a polemic against some unnamed would-be prophet or seer? Or is he in effect recommending to the reader the Sufi exercises mentioned in the paragraph which follows that will strengthen the soul, so that the person will not be overwhelmed by the visions he receives?

The truths revealed in visions are validated by the deep personal experience of their disclosure. Formal demonstration, the like of which is available in books, is a poor substitute for verifying those same truths; those who do not merit such revelations must settle for truths of that sort. The ability to receive such unveilings depends upon two variables: the weakening of the body and the strengthening of the soul. Ibn Kammūna does not say if one variable is stronger than the other. The body can be weakened by deliberately denying it sustenance, as in a fast. It is also naturally weakened in old age; according to a philosophical midrash of medieval Yemen, this is why the biblical forefathers gave their prophetic blessings at a very advanced age, shortly before their deaths.[16]

Following Ibn Sīnā again, Ibn Kammūna recognizes the capacity exercised by extraordinarily powerful souls to influence material objects lying outside the body in which these souls reside, whose proper functioning is entrusted to them.[17] These include what are generally called miracles (though Ibn Kammūna expressly does not use this term) such as causing rainfall or curing the sick, as well as less elitist, harmful forms of intervention, such as the evil eye. This phenomenon will be rejected, says Ibn Kammūna, only by adherents of yet another incorrect theory of the nature of the soul's bonding to the body, *inṭibāʿ*, or "impression." According to this theory, the soul is able to have an effect on the body in which she resides because she is impressed upon the bodily matter, and thus directs and motivates its movements and physical functioning, the way Nature (*ṭibā'*) directs and motivates the physical world, causing, according to the medieval conception, heavy bodies to sink and light bodies to rise. In this view, the soul can physically affect only the body upon which she is impressed. This monist view of the soul-body relationship is clearly unacceptable to Ibn Kammūna, who insists upon the soul's being a self-standing substance with a much looser connection to the body.[18]

It is striking that he inserts here a remark concerning the religious implications of this idea: "Supplication and repentance towards God gains for the soul the preparedness to receive guidance towards the good, just as thinking readies [the soul] to receive the overflow that activates knowledge [gnosis]." Both prayer and thinking are preparatory activities, whose purpose is to enable the one performing them to receive the necessary munificence, be it divine guidance or emanation.[19]

The notion of "powerful" souls, and the ability to strengthen one's soul by means of spiritual exercises, is quite germane to the topic at hand. Ibn Kammūna is interested not only in establishing that the soul is indestructible but in laying out as well the ultimate goal toward which the soul must strive. Prophets and Sufi gnostics (*'ārifūn*)—note that Ibn Kammūna places the two on the same plane—are able to achieve "stations" whose precise character is beyond the ken of ordinary people. Nonetheless we can all appreciate, and must all internalize, the need to free ourselves of base character traits.

In the course of this discussion, Ibn Kammūna upholds the "evil eye" as a real phenomenon, one of the things that can be effectuated by those with very powerful souls. One should not be overly surprised that someone as "rational" as Ibn Kammūna should do so. Ibn Sīnā provided a scientific explanation for the evil eye in his *al-Shifā'* (The Healing), and the discussion carried on in the Avicennan tradition.[20] I detect, however, a different slant in Ibn Kammūna's account. Whereas Ibn Sīnā explains the phenomenon fully within the extraordinary abilities of exceptionally powerful souls, Ibn Kammūna hints that the ability of this act to take effect is due at least in part to the readiness of the victim and his astonishment at the eye that is focused on him. This may be another mark of Maimonides' influence. Note that Ibn Kammūna discusses this effect along with others that are explicitly said to be due to the "readiness" of the soul.

These supernatural powers are famously associated with the Sufi "gnostics" (*'ārifūn*). In a somewhat daring gesture, Ibn Kammūna equates here these Sufi adepts and their extraordinary psychic abilities as they progress through the "stations" (*maqāmāt*) along the path with the prophets. In fact, al-Ghazālī had already proposed a daring commonality between prophets and those who had "tasted" a mystical experience.[21]

The final chapter in this section, and the culmination of the first half of the book, argues for the supremacy of intellectual pleasures over sensual ones. The reader will learn not just why this is so, but also why this feature of our existence may not be evident to everyone. Unlike the effervescent sensual pleasures, intellectual pleasures are eternal and unchanging. The latter are penetrating and liberating, the former superficial and enslaving. But someone who has never "tasted" intellectual bliss will not appreciate this, just as a deaf person cannot enjoy music.

Like all philosophers of his epoch, Ibn Kammūna places intellectual perfection at the top of the scale of available human perfections. The person who internalizes (in his intellect, of course) the cosmic order becomes quite literally a world unto himself and a living witness of the truth and goodness of the universe as a whole. Ibn Kammūna is, of course, not referring to the well-worn notion of the human as microcosm, insofar as the parts function together much as the parts of universe work together. He rather has in mind the well-ordered abstract truths and principles upon which the reality of the universe is founded, from which flow the good that suffuses the cosmos. This recalls the ideal, mentioned in the preceding chapter, of the world as macro-anthropos.

The notion of body and mind competing for the soul's attention and resources was widely held. Occupation with the body must come at the expense of intellectual endeavor; and intellectual exertion will lessen the attention given to the body's calling for its urges. There is nothing unusual in Ibn Kammūna's endorsement of this point. However, the examples that he offers are quite out of the ordinary. A person concentrating on a difficult problem is suddenly stricken with the sexual urge; however, since at least part of his mind is still pulling in the direction of intellectual activity, the sexual urge will perforce weaken. Ordinary people can suffer psychic damage by public disgrace or, alternatively, by applying themselves to an intellectual quest that is beyond their capacity to attain. These trade-offs are biological; they are based on the truism that internal feelings can overpower sensory input. As proof, Ibn Kammūna notes that an animal will feed its young, thus responding to an internal parental sense, before feeding itself, in answer to its sensible hunger.

Intellectual exertion and bodily lust draw upon the same reservoir of psychic resources. Hence someone who is dealing simultaneously with an intellectual problem and a sudden sexual urge, each of which tugs for the person's full attention, will find the lustful urge lessening, due to its competition with the intellectual effort. It seems to me that Ibn Kammūna is drawing, even if indirectly, upon the Talmudic advice (Kiddushim 30b): "If this miscreant assaults you, take him to the academy; if he is made of stone, he will melt, and if he is made of iron, he will break into pieces."

One way to get this point across more forcefully is to take as an example an act that offers both sensual and spiritual pleasure, and decide which of the two is stronger. Ibn Kammūna chooses sexual intercourse for this test; the sensual pleasure is obvious, the spiritual one, I take it, is the response of one's partner. Now take the case of necrophilia: Ibn Kammūna argues that the body derives no pleasure from that act, not even a sensual one. This proves the superiority of spiritual pleasures.

In making these points Ibn Kammūna utilizes the Arabic words *dhawq* (taste) and *shawq* (craving). Both belong to the vocabulary of the Sufis, but both also made their way into the discourse of philosophers with Sufi leanings, especially Ibn Sīnā, and theologians who chose the Sufi path, most notably al-Ghazālī.[22] Indeed, Ibn Sīnā observes that a "taste" stimulates a "craving" for more.[23] *Taste* refers to a brief, partial, but immediate experience which should stimulate the initiate's appetite for more; *craving* describes the passionate urge for closeness to God, similar to the urge of the lover for a meeting with the beloved. The sexual imagery here is deliberate. One must appeal to sensuality in order to convey the immediacy and intensity of the experience; in this brief passage, taste, the sexual urge, and the enjoyment of music are all invoked.

Finally, Ibn Kammūna promises the reader that the soul's reunion with a body will not necessarily prevent her from enjoying intellectual pleasures (including those gained in an earlier life?).

Once again, he is not forthcoming as to this intention: Is it the revivification of the dead? or is it one in a series of transmigrations? Much more could be said about the soul, her states, and her destiny. However, in order to attain these ultimate pleasures, the individual needs to do a lot of work on him- or herself. How to go about that lifelong task will be the subject of Part II.

To Establish a Group of Features (*aḥwāl*) of the Immaterial Soul, Especially What Pertains to the Precise Determination of Her Being Free [of Matter], Her Transposition After Death, the Impossibility of Her Nonexistence, and the Mode of Her Felicity and Perfection[1]

Chapter One

On how the soul is linked to the body and joined to it, her bonding to it, and her control over (*taṣarruf*) its faculties

An exhaustive discourse about soul-related questions, the division of her faculties, special properties, and actions, as well the way in which she is bound to the body, would be lengthy; moreover, it is widely available in the books that have already appeared. The most important thing that has been mentioned about this and the most accessible to comprehension is what I am setting down in this flash (*lam'a*). The first of these is to ascertain that the soul is that to which everyone points when saying, "I apprehended such and such" or "I did such and such." All of her attendant faculties are but instruments for her; otherwise an action of one of them would not be connected to the action of another, and you would not be able to say, "I sensed and so I became irritated" and "I perceived and so I moved." All the faculties of the body are under her control, for the capacity to set in motion is nothing other than [a capacity] for acquiring that which is useful or for avoiding that which is harmful, both of which trace back to her in a certain sense. The perceiving [faculty] is nothing but [a group of] spies who report news, conveying it to her; the [faculties] of representation and retention are for the purpose of retaining it; their authority is the authority of their treasurer. In this manner are all the bodily faculties when you think about them. Likewise, every organ of the body has been prepared for a purpose that derives from the soul.

More than one soul may be bound to a single body, but they would differ in their ultimate rank; and the division into ranks would end up in a single soul that is chief over all.[2] Perhaps those [lower] souls are the powers that are subservient to her. However, two souls may not be joined to a single body with a connection like that of that chief one; otherwise opposites would set in simultaneously to that one body—e.g., motion and rest or sleep and waking.

All of our perceptions and voluntary movements belong to a single soul that perceives all of the types of percepts; were it not so, then it would not be ruling in favor of some percepts against others. Indeed, that which rules for one thing against another must perceive them both simultaneously, even if her perception of one of them is by means of a bodily organ, while [her perception] of the other is without an instrument; they [the latter] are described as lust, aversion, pleasure, pain, will, ability, and action. Were the matter not so, her perception would not entail her achieving those things for herself.[3] Since those things are bound to this perception by this [particular] connection that we encounter [already] in our souls, it is innate (*fiṭriyy*), and [apparent to] to the intellect when contemplated.

Chapter Two

[153] That the soul is neither a body, nor is she a state within one; that she is simple, with no external complexity; and that she is a self-standing substance[4]

This human soul is not that perishable structure [i.e., the body], nor is she the temperament [mixture] of the body, nor is she a congruous proportion of its elements.[5] Those things are always transmuting and dissolving, even though the human person sees himself to be the same [person] that he has been for many years.[6]

She is neither this totality nor a particular organ or particular organs, to which disjointing does not make its way in the course of a lifetime, since there is not a part of the body whose state the human person does not ignore in the course of some state of self-perception. How can the same thing be perceived and not perceived while in the same state? You already know that whenever he [a person] perceives his essence, his perception of himself adds nothing to his essence; and whenever he is like this [in the state of self-perception], his essence exists so long as he perceives it. This entails that whenever the human is not paying attention to his essence while in a certain state, then he is dissimilar to his essence, and not within it, whether it be a body or bodily, or neither body nor bodily.[7]

We have already seen that everything that knows its [own] essence is simple, with no internal, extra-mental complexity. Rather, should some complexity be thought to be within it, it would [only] be due to (*biḥasbi*) mental reflection, not external reality. The human soul must be like this. She cannot be a body or a state within it [the body], an inherence (*ḥulūl*), [or a] flow (*sarayān*); otherwise she would be divided into parts by the connection.[8] But if she were divided into parts by means of the division into adjacent parts,[9] she would not receive the acquired traits (*malakāt*) that are not divided into parts in that way, such as the traits of knowledge, cleverness, bravery, cowardice, and carelessness. Instead, she would have only strengthening and weakening. Otherwise, should these or [154] similar [traits] be received by her, they would be divided according to the divisions of that within which they inhere. They would be divided into parts by division into adjacent parts, and that contradicts what has been assumed.[10]

The soul is not a state [or "condition"] within something, be it immaterial or not; otherwise that something would be self-standing, or it would trace back to that which is self-standing. Then that would be the thing to which the activities are to be ascribed, insofar as it has some accident within it, rather than [its being ascribed] to that accident [that acts?] by means of it. Don't you see that one says, "The soul acted by her ability or by will"; one does not say, "Will and ability acted by means of the soul." This is evident to everyone who can see.

Chapter Three

That the soul does not die with the death of the body, nor will she ever cease to exist

Given that there is no complexity at all in the soul, nor is she a state that inheres within a location, she therefore will not cease to exist. For whatever was *in actu,* then ceased to exist, its capacity to exist or not to exist belongs to something else; that other thing is what bears it.

Indeed, the essence (*dhāt*) of the thing, insofar as it [the thing] is *in actu,* is not *in potentia* [with regard to] its essence, though it may be *in potentia* [relative to] some other matter. An example is the power of vision which is in the eye but which is not the same as vision. Were that power within vision itself, the thing would be simultaneously *in actu* and *in potentia.*[11]

Thus, were the simple thing, within which nothing else inheres, to accept nonexistence, then it would be existing in the state for which it has been assumed to be not existing, on account of the necessity that the recipient exist when that which is received arrives.[12] Anything whose establishment entails its abolition is impossible; therefore, the nonexistence of the soul is impossible. For this reason, were one to search thoroughly through all of the existing things, one would not find something that ceases to exist other than a compound and that which is not [155] self-standing.

Now, with regard to self-standing simples: the complex disintegrates into them, but they never cease to exist. As for those [simples] that are not self-standing, you will know the status that appertains to them.

The human body, insofar as it was constituted to have a governor, which is the soul, when that constitution leaves it, on account of the causes that lead to death, the body becomes such that it does not accept this governor and its connection to it is severed.[13] However, this does not entail the nullification of the governor. The case of the decomposition of the body as a whole is just like the case of the decomposition of one its organs. Death is nothing but a general passing away (*zamāna*) for all of the organs. The destruction of the instrument does not entail the nonexistence of the one who operated it.[14]

The simple does not emanate, from the aspect of its simplicity, from the compound, when its complexity is considered; because if one of its [the compound's] parts were in itself sufficient for causation, then the rest would have no effect. However, if it were not sufficient in itself, then it would affect the thing as a caused being (*min al-maʿlūl*), in which case the caused being would [also] be compound. If it has no effect at all, then it has no point of entry into causality.[15]

The form of the grouping is one of the components of the complex, and it has its own rule.[16] Whatever emanates from a complex has within it a duality, something which, however, does not prevent its root essence (*dhāt aṣliyya*) from being one.[17] Hence the simple essence of the soul, even if it is contingent, is caused by a simple essence whose ranking in reality does not fall short of that of the soul, because the soul's knowledge of her essence does not add anything to her essence. It is a perfection for the essence insofar as she is [what she is].[18] Since the efficient cause [of the soul] has this essential perfection, it is not allowed to fall short of it with regard to it. Whatever derives from the perfect active agent (*al-fāʿil al-tāmm al-fāʿiliyya*) is like a shadow for it; it is not more complete and perfect than it.[19] But the perfection that follows upon the essence [not an essential perfection, but rather a secondary one] may be acquired from something that is not her [the essence's] efficient [cause]; in this it differs from the case of the very essence (*nafs al-dhāt*).[20]

It has therefore been established that there exist simple, immaterial [beings] that are more perfect than the human souls with respect to knowledge and life. They are the efficient causes of the souls; you may call them angels, intellects, or some other name. The soul can cease to exist only if her simple cause ceased to exist; to speak about the nonexistence of that which is her cause is the same as speaking about her [own] nonexistence. But this would lead to the nonexistence of the First Necessary, so greatly exalted above that is He!

The soul and her causes both proximate and remote will not cease to exist.[21] How could it be otherwise? She will not annihilate her own essence. No given existence can annihilate her by disabling an entry point for her [the soul's] existence—that [given reality] would be an opposite—because it has no abode (*maḥall*), from which the opposite can deter it. Nor will she be nullified [156] by that whose absence is an entry point for her nonexistence, and that would be a precondition (*sharṭ*).[22] Given the permanence of the cause that mandates her existence, the absence of that which separates her does not bring about her nonexistence, nor [is there any effect on the part of] that which separates her.

Accidents that oppose her perfection do not detract from her perception of her own essence, which [perception] does not add anything to her essence.[23] The change and variation of her accidents in their being a perfection or defect for her has no effect with regard to bringing about her annihilation, because the permanence of that which avails her existence requires that she never be removed from existence and that she not be annihilated. The dissolution (*inḥilāl*)[24] is a certain motion that traces back to the heavenly motions, just as it has been determined in the well-known books.[25]

When it is stated that the configuration (*hay'a*) or the accident has ceased to exist, this refers to the [cessation of the] bonding to a certain abode in which they are manifest; however, the bonding to the agent is not annihilated, and hence they may become manifest in a different abode.

The transposition that is forbidden to accidents is only the transposition that would be required for their independence in reality, or in the directions, or in local motion, and whatever follows their course. However, their transposition in the sense that their cause (literally, "agent") makes them apparent to sensation or to some other abode, and then, in a similar manner, makes them apparent in abode different from that [first] abode, like the form that appears in a mirror but is not really in it—that is not forbidden. Perhaps all the accidents that you know of have only had their abode made manifest in this way.[26]

Annihilation from its abode in this manner is not true annihilation. As long the bounty of the Necessary necessitates its emanation upon it, it will not be annihilated in the sense of having its true reality removed from existence. Instead, it may possibly be annihilated in the sense of not being present to sensation, or to an abode in which it manifests itself, or from a thing to which it can be connected, and thus it distances itself from it by means of some motion, as is the case with the dissolution of compounds; or in some other sense that follows this trajectory.

Whoever looks into the wisdom in the creation of man and ascertains that which has been shown and clarified concerning the Creator's watching over His creations, and His mercy upon them will notice that the final purpose to be sought after in his having been created is not something transient; and the sweeter it [the final purpose] is, [157] the more bitter is the fear of its going away. There is no final purpose that is proper for the likes of this Wise One—mighty is His rule! But the final purpose [for humans] is an everlasting felicity. Therefore, the human must have an enduring soul, which is not the same as this mortal structure. Indeed, this structure is expertly made, and these wondrous things have been created in it, but only in order that it serve it as an instrument for attaining perfection.

This is an intuitive argument (*hujja hadsiyya*). Perhaps someone who does not find this intuition within himself may find it useful. The dependable proof for it has been given in the preceding.

Chapter Four

On the perfection of the soul, and her falling short; and the manner of her coming into contact with the highest world and acquiring items of knowledge from it; and a note on a group of her special properties and effects

If we were to limit our consideration to her essence, the human soul has no life other than perceiving her own essence. But [her] perceiving other things and her actions as well are [effectuated] by means of the bodily faculties and her intellectual capacities. [In order to do this] they require something to take them from potentiality to actuality. Therefore, her life without these things is a defective life.[27] Awareness (*shuʿūr*) of existence is felicity, and among the existing things some are superior to others.[28] The most noble of them is the First Existence.[29] Felicities range in gradation according to what can be gained from these existing things. But it is impossible for an essence to be free of the shadow of the First's falling upon it. That [First Existence] is the true light; everything else reflects its light. The immaterial beings range in gradation according to the range of gradation in the illumination of its light upon them; and the range of gradation of their delights in its perception [i.e., of the First Existence] is similar to the range in gradation in that perception.

Proximity to the essence of the percept is determined by the strength of the perception of it.[30] The separate immaterial beings range in their delight according to the range of their nearness or distance from the Necessary. In this [same] way the ranks of the souls and their grades differ with regard to nobility or baseness.

The soul's engagement with the bodily faculties diverts her from addressing the Highest Excellency as well as from receiving items of knowledge from Him.[31] You may ascertain this upon reflecting upon those things concerning which information is received in dreams: this is so only because of the fewness of its tasks, since the soul has left her occupation with the external senses. The information is not due to thinking, since humans [158] are quite capable of thinking during their waking state. Hence it is due only to the soul's linking up with the supernal sources which bestow upon it that hidden thing, on account of the fewness of her bodily tasks.

The link between the soul and the Highest Excellency may, however, intensify, so that she is informed about hidden matters even in a state of wakefulness, especially when the soul is powerful and sufficient to counterbalance the aspects [of bodily life] that attract her to the body, so that it does not distract her from linking up to the above-mentioned sources. Prophetic narratives are due to this cause. But for the person whose soul is not strong, that [dream or vision] may lead to his senses being startled and his imagination perturbed; perhaps his senses and imagination were like that in their original makeup. That is a deficiency which is not praiseworthy.

When the weakness of the bodily impediment combines with the strength of the soul, whether this [strength] be inborn or is acquired, the way that the soul is strengthened by training (*tadrīb*) or the exercise (*riyāḍa*) ascribed to the [Sufi] gnostics—then the contact may be so fortified that the soul obtains many hidden things, venerable items of knowledge and illuminating pleasures, whose true nature (*kunh*) is perceived by a person only on his own. Whoever doesn't find them [on his own] must believe in them on the support of their evidence (*bi-qiyām adillatihā*); at the very least, he should not deny them simply because they do not exist for him. The soul may also be so fortified as to have an effect on another body [other than the one in which she resides], as in the case of bringing down rain, removing illnesses, producing earthquakes, and the like. This will be rejected only by the person who thinks that the soul has an effect on the body only because she is impressed (*inṭabaʿa*) in it.[32]

Harming by means of the eye belongs to this class, and it is empirically verified. Its cause is a special property possessed by some souls to enervate whosoever is stricken with wonder by them. Supplication and repentance towards God gain for the soul the preparedness to receive guidance towards the good, just as thinking readies [the soul] to receive the overflow that activates knowledge [gnosis]. Magic is one of the effects of the soul [literally, "psychic effects"]. Many strange things about the soul are known by repeated experience, their recurrence, and by some sort of reasoning (*qiyās*).[33] Often it is difficult for us to corral or represent to ourselves the "stations" of the gnostics, be they prophets or not. But whoever is evil and does not refine his soul, why then the power of his soul is not to be praised because he relies upon it to bring about the bad rather than the good. Base character traits are a tremendous barrier in the face of linkage with the higher world and the acquisition of the supreme felicity because they incline the soul towards [159] the side of the body. She is thus prevented from linking up with the location of felicity so long as the soul is stained by them, regardless of whether she is joined to the body or free of it.

However, the soul [when] joined to this body is blocked from the true realities of things, not because she is impressed upon it [the body], but because of her being occupied with it, and her being aroused to its lusts and desires until they are satisfied. This arousal and lust is a disposition of the soul which is firmly embedded and consolidated within us. Should this consolidation take hold after the separation [from the body], then her status after separation is just like her status beforehand, unless those dispositions leave her by means of a removing agent that we do not recognize.[34] If the soul detaches from the body and does not attach herself to another one, its cognizance of her own essence is not mixed with her cognizance of the body; then she is most fulfilled. Likewise, her intelligibles are more intensely abstract, for we cannot intellectualize anything while we are bodily without some phantasm [imagination], or something like a phantasm, being coupled to it. When this flaw is removed, the enjoyment of the soul in its life is most perfect.[35]

Chapter Five

On pleasure and pain, showing that the intellectual [varieties] of both are more powerful than the sensual ones

Intellectual perception is more perfect than the sensual [variety] because it is better, more perfect, longer lasting, greater, and surer of arrival at the percept;[36] hence its pleasure is more fulfilling. The special perfection of the rational soul from the aspect of its intellectual faculty is that it becomes an intellectual cosmos within which are inscribed the form of the all, along with the intellectualized order within it and the good that flows onto it. He then is a counterpart to the real world in its entirety, and a witness to that which is absolutely beautiful and good. This is better and more perfect than the perfections of the other faculties, such as carnal appetite, anger, imagination, memory, and the others.

Indeed, they are incommensurable with it in terms of excellence, perfection, plenitude, and the rest of whatever makes taking pleasure in percepts complete.[37] Moreover, how can the endurance of the eternal be commensurate with the endurance of the perishable and changeable? How can the status of that which can manage to meet only with surfaces be [compared to] that which penetrates the core of the percept?[38] And how [160] can perception be compared to perception, and percept to percept?[39] Indeed, intellect has a greater number of percepts than does sensation; it is more powerfully accomplished (*ashadd taqḍiyy^{an}*) on the perceiver, divesting him of excesses and plunging into both his interior and [his] exterior.[40]

The preoccupations with the body stand in the way of longing for that perfection in a way consistent with its ultimate attainment. For the occupation of the soul with sensibles prevents her from turning towards the intelligibles. She finds no "taste" of them, nor does she attain any craving for them, just as an impotent person has no desire for intercourse and the deaf person has no desire to hear melodies.[41] Think about this: when the noble of soul applies himself to a problem that concerns him but then is seized by lust so that he wavers between the two extremes—in that case, the lust is lightened. Common souls may also be affected by pains and degrading damages on account of mental exertion or craving for an intellectual matter. Internal pleasures, even when they are not intellectual, are more powerful than external sensory ones. Contemplate this with regard to the preference an animal has for its young over itself with regard to food and other things.

I say: The pleasure of intercourse attains power to such an extent not only because it is sensual but because of a spiritual notion that the soul perceives in the partner. For this reason, the body does not take pleasure in the copulation with a corpse, on the assumption that its visually perceived form will not change.[42] For this reason [also], the pleasure in sexual union with one person is stronger than it is with another, even though the gratification of lust achieved thereby is equal. Hence intercourse is a combination of two pleasures, sensual and spiritual. But the share of the spiritual in pleasure is stronger than that of the sensual. No one will prefer sensual pleasure over an intellectual one unless his soul is as low and ruined as can be, or he does not distinguish between the intellectual and the nonintellectual.

If the soul joins [again] to a body after death, as it is in the afterlife accepted in the true religions, or with some other body, celestial or terrestrial, this would not necessarily bar her from receiving intellectual pleasures or pains along with the sensual pleasures and pains that she attains due to her joining to a body.[43]

I do not see any reason to say more than this about the states of the soul and her destiny; it [what I have already said] is the most important and most necessary for the purpose of this summary. Beyond this are many inquiries; mentioning some and leaving out the rest is better than the opposite for the requirements of that which we are involved in here.[44] However, since true felicity is not fully realized without the improvement of the practical faculty, I will follow up with an account of useful principles about that. Protection and help are from God!

PART II.
ON PRACTICE
FIRST GATE

Synopsis and Commentary

Praxis begins with *tawba*—not simple repentance, in the sense of acknowledging past failings and resolving to abandon them, but rather a resolute decision to return to God. Anyone, even the master, can have a moment of forgetfulness, from which he must recover. Repentance is essentially resolve, a personal decision and commitment. The voyagers (*sālikūn*) on the path to personal refinement begin their quest with an act of repentance. *Sālikūn* is a common Sufi term which denotes spiritual travelers, wayfarers on the road to spiritual perfection.[1] Medieval philosophers were of one mind that all change takes place in the recipient when it is properly formatted to receive an external stimulus. Such is the case with repentance as well: it is effectuated when the heart takes on the proper disposition that will allow it to receive "the lights of knowledge."

The opening sentence in this section is taken verbatim from al-Ghazālī's *al-Arba'īn fī Uṣūl al-Dīn* (The Forty Principles of Religion).[2] The same idea is expressed in a longer sentence at the beginning of part four of the same author's *Iḥyā' 'Ulūm al-Dīn* (The Revival of the Religious Sciences). Much of the ethics in this section derives from the former work, which is an abridgment of the *Iḥyā'*.

This theoretical statement is followed immediately by a remark concerning the role of the body. Bodily forms of worship can be useful in directing knowledge to the heart; acts of worship done with the body are likened to the capital with which one starts a business. Supererogatory acts then follow just as profits follow upon a good investment of capital. I believe that Ibn Kammūna is thinking mainly of prayer, with its formalized and ritualized bodily movements and posture (especially in Islamic worship) as well as spontaneous gestures (characteristic of Jewish prayer). However, other religious acts, such as the giving of charity, certainly fit his description. There may be a subtext here as well; Ibn Kammūna may be hinting to the initiate that first and foremost he must be scrupulous about formal religious performances.

An almost identical idea is expressed by Baḥya Ibn Paquda, the eleventh-century Jewish writer from Saragossa, near the end of the introduction to his Sufism-infused *Guide to the Duties of the Heart:* "My purpose here is to reveal the principles of our religion that are embedded in limpid intellects, and the poles of our law that are ensconced in our souls. When we set our minds to them, their verity becomes clarified in our conscience, and their lights manifest themselves in our bodily limbs."[3]

Ibn Kammūna's idea resonates with that of Baḥya, but this does not mean that he was at all influenced by the latter's book. Indeed, although Jewish thinkers had for generations been attracted to Sufi thought and practice, there is only a tenuous link between the different manifestations of "Jewish Sufism" in al-Andalus, Egypt, and Iraq.[4] The "Jewish Sufis" in Egypt, among them the direct descendants of Maimonides, rarely cite Baḥya and never Yehuda ha-Levi. Ibn Kammūna, the sole representative of Iraqi-Jewish pietism (or, at least, the only one known to scholarship), drew heavily on ha-Levi's theology for his *Tanqīḥ*, but his Sufi ideas betray no connection to Jewish sources. When dealing with pietism, the shared values are such that it is not always necessary or helpful to look for specific sources.

In any event, "parallels" are not hard to uncover. Similar notions concerning bodily movements are found, for example, in the writings of the ninth-century scholar al-Tirmidhī.[5] Bodily gestures similar to those mentioned by Ibn Kammūna are known also from other, pre-Islamic cultures.[6]

The chief offense is love of this world. In order to free ourselves from this, we need to reduce engagement with bodily needs to the barest minimum. This is best done—most effectively and most sincerely—by a mental gesture which recognizes and internalizes the vanity of this world. However, there are those who only superficially reduce their involvement with pleasures; their real hope is to secure those very material pleasures in the next world. This is wrong.

This world and the next are adversaries, and the soul can give her undivided attention to only one of the two. Again, this calls for mental resolve. We must always be conscious that whatever sensory delights may exist, they are here only for the purpose of maintaining our finite, terrestrial existence. Put differently—but without doing violence to Ibn Kammūna's idea—pleasures are the trappings of bodily necessities; they serve no end in themselves. A person cannot be on intimate terms with his body and at the same time keep it out of his heart.

In explaining why involvement with this-worldly worries necessarily detracts from the soul's attention to her spiritual tasks, Ibn Kammūna speaks of the soul's being busy with one thing (*ishtaghalat bi-shay'in*) as the activity that prevents her engaging in something else. I do not think that he is denying the soul's ability to multi-task. It seems here that *ishtighāl* parallels in a way the psychological state of self-awareness; it has more the sense of "immersion" than of "occupation." In moments of self-awareness, the soul (and self, and person) is immersed in the immaterial "next" world, in a deathless dimension. But when the soul turns her attention to this world, she must then have a lapse in her self-awareness.

The technical language of psychology (*'ilm al-nafs*) is not applicable in this section, whose subject is praxis. Though the language is different, I think that Ibn Kammūna remains totally consistent with the notions of self-awareness that he advances in the first section of the *Kalimāt.* Even when attending to activities that are vital to maintaining ourselves in this world, the attention of the soul should be inwards, not directed to the body but to herself, or to the next world—it amounts to the same thing, in my understanding.[7]

Ibn Kammūna is ambivalent about the place of social life. Like so many contemplative thinkers, he sees great value in isolation and abandoning all social goals. However, he also sees benefits in mixing with people. He is not here following Maimonides, who concedes, following Aristotle, that man is a "political animal"—that is to say, one of the creatures whose biology naturally requires them to live in groups. Instead, he can see real benefits in social interaction beyond the basic necessities of food, clothing, and shelter. Each of us must decide whether to join in on a case-by-case basis, "according to the person and the situation."

This is true for the person already advanced along the path. For the ignorant, however, interaction is a necessity. Ibn Kammūna sees *dhikr*, a social activity of Sufis as well as a religious-ethical performance, and other practices undertaken collectively by initiates to the spiritual path to be of unmistakable utility.

Satan may call on you to do something good, only to lure you into something bad. In some cases, both acts are good, but one is to be preferred over the other. In these cases, Satan is inviting you to perform the good act so as to keep you from performing the one that is even better. This is the issue known in Islamic thought as *al-mafḍūl* (a good act) and *al-fāḍil* (a better one, the one to be preferred). A classic example is the following: it may be the call of Satan that beckons us to perform supererogatory prayers because that activity comes at the expense of a higher good, such as seeking knowledge. However, Ibn Kammūna chooses a different example: the anger that surges in people under the illusion that they are wreaking God's vengeance. That too is the work of the devil.

Satan's reach extends to theology and metaphysics. For example, Satan lies behind the denial of immaterial entities on the grounds that we cannot imagine how they exist; imagination is here doing the devil's work. In this idea, as in so many others in this chapter in particular, Ibn Kammūna is building upon the Sufi manual written by the Ishrāqī martyr Shihāb al-Dīn al-Suhrawardī.[8]

The next two chapters discuss protective measures: Chapter Two, measures against sinning with the body and the tongue in particular, and the far longer Chapter Three, measures to guard against "scourges of the heart." Ibn Kammūna begins with a general observation: it is harder to refrain from transgressions than it is to perform positive commandments. Our bodies and faculties are God's gift to us; we should not use them against Him.

Restrain the eye from looking at things that are forbidden or from gazing upon anyone with scorn. Don't let your ears admit slander and indecency. But above all, the tongue must be reined in. It is speech that distinguishes man from animals, and, therefore, speech should be used with great discretion.

Ibn Kammūna observes that "speech was intended only so that a person may know what is in his friend's soul" Human beings alone have the ability to speak. Aristotle says that we have been given that ability by nature so that we can speak and reason with each other in order to distinguish right from wrong, good from bad, and just from unjust. Would it be overenthusiastic to suggest that Ibn Kammūna has perhaps anticipated Jürgen Habermas, who quipped: "Reaching understanding is the inherent telos of human speech"? For these reasons, we must not lie or break a promise that has been made. We should not insult or quarrel. Do not praise yourself or curse anyone else.

Put in your belly only permitted food. In giving this maxim, Ibn Kammūna is once again careful not to make it community-specific. Philosophically minded people from all communities agree that a person's intake should be below the point of satiety. This holds true for sexual activity as well. A final piece of advice: "Keep your hands from hurting anyone with them, keep your feet from running after something forbidden, or going to any wrongdoing; this is what you must watch over in what concerns your exterior limbs."

I call attention to the nondenominational character of the list of injunctions regarding food, drink, and sexual behavior. Jews,

Muslims, Christians, Buddhists, and Pythagoreans all observe restrictions on the types of food that they eat. The same communities may restrict sexual activity in different ways, but all agree on limiting it in some way; indeed, there exist differences among subgroups within these larger communities. Whatever is forbidden to you, urges Ibn Kammūna, do not indulge in it.

Chapter Three addresses the scourges that are particular to the heart—the heart serving here as the locus of mental, psychic, and spiritual activity. This usage is similar, but not quite identical, to the role(s) assigned to the heart in the Bible or in Sufi thought. Ibn Kammūna identifies the heart as *'ayn al-nafs,* which I translate as "the eye of the soul." *'Ayn* may also mean "quintessence," which fits the context quite well. Nonetheless, I think that "eye" may be more appropriate here. In medieval Islamic and Jewish philosophy, the "inner" eye is more commonly referred to as the eye of the heart. Students of the *Theology of Aristotle,* a fairly widely read compendium drawn from the work of Plotinus, would have recognized the term "eye of the soul." This source is especially important for Ibn Kammūna on account of its assigning to the "eye of the soul" a role in the acquisition of knowledge. We read there that "when the soul wishes to know something, it casts its eye over it, then returns to its own essence."[9] Paul the Persian, in his *Introduction to Logic,* which is cited by Ibn Kammūna's contemporary Bar Hebraeus, remarks that the eye of the soul is "the only true eye that sees everything, because of its affinity with the truth that resides in everything."[10]

Ibn Kammūna goes on to say that the heart is like the king or commander-in-chief of the all the bodily organs; this notion sounds very much like the hegemonikon of the Stoics, which they located in the brain. It functions as the warehouse of a person's "precious jewel" (soul, self, identity?), along with intellect, knowledge of God and all wisdom, and noble character traits. For all of these reasons, the heart must be kept sound and clean.

The first afflictions of the heart that are mentioned are longing for immortality or fear of death, envy, and haste or impatience. Ibn Kammūna singles out "prolonged hope" (*ṭūl al-amal*), again following al-Ghazālī, who in his discussion of *tawakkul*, "reliance"—a section of his book thoroughly exploited by Ibn Kammūna in the *Kalimāt*—notes that "prolonged hope harms reliance."[11] The constant remembrance of our mortality and our inevitable demise appears frequently in Sufi writings. It is the theme of the concluding chapter of al-Ghazali's *Iḥyā'*.

These notions are given a few sentences. Ibn Kammūna then moves on to a longer disquisition on pride and the related vices of grandeur and eminence. (We shall soon see that these belong properly to the deity; because of a certain isomorphism between the human and divine, they are found in the former as well.) Anger is difficult to cure; vanity is one of its chief causes.

Scourges of the heart that have to do with money and material wealth are given much more space. Whatever wealth we acquire in the course of a lifetime has been given by God to allow us to meet our religious and civil obligations. People should not accumulate wealth in order to pass it on to their descendants. If the children are good, God will provide for them as well; but if they are evil, then their inheritance will support their sins. Hence people ought to disburse what remains of their fortune to the needy.

Love of honor is worse than love of money. Yet people naturally desire honor, and the reason for this is that honor is one of the divine attributes. Herein lies a great secret of the human condition and its implications for ethics; it is the isomorphism mentioned above. There does exist some "relationship" between the human spirit and the deity; they are not absolutely dissimilar. For this very reason we find in humans the "divine" urge to rule or master, if only by mastering through the instrument of knowledge—the only way that humans may master the heavens. For this same reason, there is something in the human imagination that leads us to picture ourselves ruling over other people; and this causes humans to wish their fame to spread as well.

The passage on honor (*jāh*) is taken from the chapter on the same vice (though ideally a virtue, as explained in the text) from al-Ghazālī's *al-Arbaʿīn*.[12] There are some direct citations, including the opening sentence. The closing sentences, beginning with "A reasonable person knows that even if all of the people on earth were to bow down to him, neither the one bowing nor the one bowed to is permanent," do not have precise counterparts in al-Ghazālī's book, but they continue in very much the spirit of his discussion. The same ideas are expounded at much greater length in al-Ghazālī's *Iḥyāʾ*.[13]

Note that Ibn Kammūna—following his source—speaks here of the human spirit (*rūḥ*) as bearing some relationship to the divine; in the section on the soul, he speaks exclusively of the soul (*nafs*) or her essence/self (*dhāt*). Al-Ghazālī uses *rūḥ* because his claim that the spirit has something divine (*amr ilāhī*) is a play on words on the Qur'anic verse (17:85) he cites.[14] Ibn Kammūna omits the Qur'anic citation—I suggest that he does so not just for the sake of brevity but in keeping with his effort to make this treatise religiously neutral. Nonetheless, the terminological inconsistency does not bother him.

The idea here is that the human spirit, having something in common with the divine, is naturally endowed with honor.

Al-Ghazālī adds that as a rule people suppress this trait; the Pharaoh of the biblical book of Exodus is the notable exception. Hence it is natural for people to desire to rule over others. In the edition of al-Ghazālī that I consulted, it is the person seeking fame and power who wants to control others by means of his own heart. However, the copy that Ibn Kammūna saw (or the common source, if one is to be supposed, and I regard this as unlikely) may have displayed the text as it stands in the *Kalimāt*.

High standing is not in itself a vice. Seeking after true perfection may yield worthy prestige. However, if a man stalls at the lower stations in the quest for perishable glory, then that is blameworthy. The small measure of pride or self-esteem that protects us against abuse ought to suffice.

Inspirational manuals and ethical handbooks of the period, without any exception known to me, rail against hypocrisy. It seems that the practice of feigning devotion, histrionics with religious association, was widespread. The *Kalimāt* is no exception in denouncing manifestations of piety aimed at impressing people. People ought to worship in private and remove any thought of public accolade from their minds. Drawing on an imperative that is at least as ancient as the biblical book of Proverbs, Ibn Kammūna warns against taking false or unnecessary oaths.

The chapter ends with an explanation based on the science of the time relating ethical behavior to the "configuration" (*hay'a*) of the soul.

Hay'a is the spatial arrangement of the components, each with its own physical qualities and characteristics; the behavior of the compound is generally a function of its configuration. In astronomy this holds true for the set of orbs whose configuration governs the motion of each planet; similarly, the configuration of the set of physical components (humors and other organic material) that together form bodily organs such as the heart and liver is responsible for each organ's particular needs, performance, and health in a given individual. Similarly, the soul was thought to have a certain configuration, from which the behavior associated with character traits issued almost mechanically.

The "*hay'a* of the soul" is often translated as "disposition," but I think that "configuration" is more precise, as the Arabic term denotes the proper arrangement of components, just as the configuration of the heavens is the proper arrangement of the celestial bodies.

The notion that actions issue forth almost mechanically from a configuration of the soul is expounded as early as tenth-century philosopher and historian Miskawayh in his *Tahdhhīb al-Akhlāq* (Refinement of Moral Character); in the perfectly just individual, justice issues forth from "a cultured, psychic configuration (*hay'a nafsaniyya adabiyya*).[15] Indeed, Miskawayh (and he is not alone) thinks of the soul as being in eternal circular motion, just like the heavenly bodies. The analogy between the *hay'a* of the heavens and the *hay'a* of the soul is deeper than we might think.

Do we have control over this configuration? Can we configure our soul so that only behavior associated with virtues will result? The issue was not fully resolved. Ibn Kammūna lets on that a person may acquire a character trait by means of habituation. I believe that here too he is following Maimonides, who dealt with the issue on several occasions, especially in his "Eight Chapters," the popular name for the long introduction he wrote to the tractate Avot as part of his commentary to the Mishnah. There Maimonides opines that by habituation—that is, repeatedly performing a task such as dispersing funds—we can "tweak" the configuration that left to itself would result in stinginess.[16]

Chapter Four of the *Kalimāt* describes the "stations" that the seeker—here qualified as the seeker after worship and knowledge—must climb through. Some of the terms that figure in the chapter title call for further explanation. "Stations," *maqāmāt* (singular: *maqāma*), are stages in moral refinement and spiritual progress that show themselves in behavior and attitude. *Maqāma* is a Sufi term; note that Ibn Kammūna speaks here specifically about stages in the individual's quest for two things: worship and knowledge. This chapter has a deep Sufi tinge to it; several passages again are nearly literal citations from some Sufi manuals written by the martyred philosopher and mystic al-Suhrawardī.

But why must the individual travel a long and difficult path in order to arrive at worship? Isn't it enough to enter the nearest mosque, synagogue, or church, or, alternatively, to find a quiet corner in one's own home or a peaceful spot in the garden and recite prayers that are readily available? Clearly, this is not the case. Worship is (among other things) an attitude. The Arabic term, *'ibāda,* means literally "servitude." True, prayer meetings are also called "services" in English, but the English term does not capture at all the sense that the Arabic aims at, which is a servile attitude: the attitude of utter dependence upon and submission to the master, along with the consciousness that the worshipper is entirely at the master's mercy. It involves, then, an attitude of complete surrender—and *islām* literally means "surrender." Internalizing this attitude requires a great deal of effort and training. It goes hand in hand with the quest for knowledge because knowledge of the cosmos, the deity, and the individual's place in the cosmos will yield the proper servile attitude needed for worship.

In Ibn Kammūna's account, the first of these stations is *tawakkul,* generally translated "reliance"; but as is often the case, a single-word translation gives only a weak approximation of the full semantic field covered by the term. Islamic thinkers debated the limits of *tawakkul.* If taken too far, as some early personalities were reported to have done, a person could simply do nothing to provide for himself, or go to an even farther extremity and venture out into the habitats of wild animals, "relying" on God for sustenance and protection. Moreover, according to the kalam, God is the only Agent; quite literally, people can do nothing, so why should they try? Ibn Kammūna endorses a compromise: the fact that God is the only "real" Agent does not absolve us of the need to look after ourselves, nor does it utterly nullify any causal connection between our actions and their results. Instead, we ought to combine a belief in human causal agency with "faith in [divine] kindness, goodness, and wisdom."

Ibn Kammūna's position—namely that with the proper attitude towards divine beneficence, allowing some sort of extra-divine causality does not harm reliance (*tawakkul*)—should be compared with the statement of al-Ghazālī in his *al-Arbaʿīn:* "The true nature of reliance calls for unicity (*tawḥīd*) in the action, but it does not call for annihilation within the unicity of the Essence. Instead, the one relying (*al-mutawakkil*) may see a multiplicity of causes and effects. Nevertheless, he must testify to the connection of the chain to its Cause."[17] In the corresponding section of the *Iḥyāʾ* (on *tawakkul*) al-Ghazālī presents a much more elaborate discussion of *tawḥīd:* its different levels, its connection to *tawakkul,* and what can be expected of people who have reached different levels of revelation (*kashf, mukāshafa*). The connections drawn here between *tawakkul,* causality, and *tawḥīd* certainly exhibit the influence of al-Ghazālī, but the exposition in the *Kalimāt* displays Ibn Kammūna's own coherent thoughts on the matter.

Theodicy also enters into the discussion. Should one think there to be some evil or defect in the world—note that Ibn Kammūna is speaking of our perceiving evil, as does Maimonides, rather than acknowledging the existence of evil—then we ought to believe that some greater good will come out of it. For example, a bitter medicine can cure a dangerous disease. In sum, we ought to train ourselves to be content with whatever God sends our way.

Contentedness (*riḍā'*) is an acquired trait (*malaka*), something we must work at in order to achieve it and assimilate it into our personality. Pourjavady and Schmidtke again find the source of this definition in al-Suhrawardī's Sufi writings. *Riḍā'* is a key concept in Islamic religiosity and ethics; it is also excruciatingly difficult to find a precise or even good English equivalent. When referring to human gestures or actions aimed at the deity, *riḍā'* is best translated by the somewhat archaic English phrase "finding favor." As a human ethical trait, it means "satisfaction" or "contentedness," but with a nuance of apathy: being content with whatever God sends our way. We should not react angrily but rather contemplate the divine machinations behind the event. The idea expressed here by Ibn Kammūna is elaborated in different language by al-Ghazālī.[18]

Ibn Kammūna next talks about a pair of concepts, fear (*khawf*) and hope (*rajā'*). In Sufi thought, the person oscillates between these two poles; each serves as a check on the other. Significantly, Ibn Kammūna begins this section with the maxim "The beginning of wisdom is fear of God," a verse from Proverbs, in the writ sacred to Jews and Christians, and also a hadith ensconced in the Islamic canon. I have already suggested that citations such as this constitute a deliberate attempt to ground his ethic in all three traditions. A bit later there is another, albeit weaker, allusion to Scripture (Ecclesiastes 11). Illustrating what he means by vain hope, Ibn

Kammūna mentions the person who does not sow, yet hopes for a crop. The truly hopeful person will do all that he can do as a farmer (or any other trade) and only then hope that God will bless his efforts with success.

Divine mercy and divine anger are another pair of opposites that figure in this discussion; clearly the former ties into hope, the latter into fear. I do not know how aware Ibn Kammūna may have been of the full pedigree of this pair. The concluding chapter of al-Ghazālī's magisterial *Iḥyā'* (of which *al-Arbaʿīn* is a very concise summary) is devoted to the profuseness (*siʿa*) of God's mercy. There we find the hadith that is reflected in Ibn Kammūna's text: "On Resurrection Day God will take out a book from beneath the Throne, in which [one finds], 'My Mercy precedes My anger, and I am the most merciful of the merciful.'" The two human emotional states, fear (*khawf*) and hope (*rajā'*), which are developed by the Sufis into ethical virtues, correlate to the two divine attributes of anger and mercy: divine anger inspires fear, and divine mercy gives hope. The Jewish roots of the distinction between divine justice and mercy were briefly explored a century ago by Ignác (Ignaz) Goldziher; the topic deserves a thorough study of its own, not just of the sources, but of the developments within Judaism (especially proto-Kabbalah) and Islam (especially Sufism), which parallel each other to a remarkable extent.[19]

The upshot of this section is that we must come to recognize and to realize—by realization I mean making it a part of our conscious reality—that all good in the world is a direct result of divine intent, whereas evil is only a byproduct of divine munificence.

The next station is thanks. Ibn Kammūna again draws upon al-Suhrawardī for the definition of this virtue; it is a surge of consciousness within the individual that he has been blessed, a surge that ignites the faculty of speech to offer audible thanks. We must be careful to offer thanks to God alone, not to be misled into thinking that the various agents of the divine deserve thanks. Where thanks are incumbent, as in the case of parents, they should be given "only out of pure, religiously prescribed devotion."

Discussion of divine goodness segues into the topic of giving thanks; and the notion of thanks leads to that of love. Such is the flow of ideas in this chapter. Perfection—clearly the intent is God, the perfect being—must not be loved on account of benefits that we obtain from it, but rather for its own sake. "Perfection is loved on its own account, and all perfection, beauty, and brilliance in existence derive from God's perfection, beauty, and brilliance."

Love of God, one of the goals of the spiritual life, is explored by means of analogies to light, color, and knowledge. The thrust of this passage on love fits in part the connection drawn by al-Ghazālī between love and knowledge, treated in a book-length study by Binyamin Abrahamov.[20] The appeal to color, as well as the notion of the intensity of light hiding color and blinding us to the divine majesty, resonate with al-Ghazālī's *Mishkāt al-Anwār* (Niche of Lights), especially this passage, essentially a gloss on the "Light Verse" of the Qur'an: "light is a form that lies behind all color, and is apprehended with color, insomuch that, so to speak, through its intense union with the colors it is not apprehended, and through its intense obviousness it is invisible. And it may be that this very intensity is the cause of its invisibility, for things that go beyond one extreme pass over to the extreme opposite."[21] These ideas of al-Ghazālī may have influenced al-Suhrawardī, another thinker upon whose work Ibn Kammūna drew extensively, as we have already seen.[22]

The section ends with a short chapter offering sage advice as to how to improve our character traits. To begin with, we must aim to ameliorate all deficiencies of character; vices are bound one to the other, so that leaving some intact will ultimately affect the entire character perversely. Ibn Kammūna then, following Maimonides who followed al-Fārābī, urges the adept to aim for the middle ground between pairs of opposing vices. Next follows a catalogue: five pairs of traits that relate to urges, and eleven pairs that relate to the intellect. Rare indeed is the individual who can achieve perfection. Fortunately, salvation does not demand utter perfection. We must all strive instead "to incline towards a beautiful internal form."

In this chapter Ibn Kammūna invokes the four virtues identified in Plato's *Republic,* usually called wisdom, courage, moderation, and justice; Ibn Kammūna's direct source, as noted by Pourjavady and Schmidtke, is one of al-Suhrawardī's Sufi writings.[23] We tend to think of justice as a social virtue, the proper regulation of individuals as they live out their lives within society. However, Plato, followed by many philosophers, considered justice a virtue of a person's individual personality.[24] Each person ought to configure his or her character traits so that they are just, that is, fixed more or less in the middle ground between two extremes. This is the "golden mean" for which Maimonides is famous; his ethics, however, owe a great deal to al-Farābī, as Herbert Davidson has shown.[25]

The First Gate, Recording a Bundle About the Improvement of the State of the Soul, Her Management, and Correcting Her Morals

Chapter One

On repentance, worship, and abstention, and what appertains to them

Know that repentance is the starting point of the "voyagers" and the key to the felicity of the initiates.[1] It is a phrase which expresses the soul's hurting on account of the demerits that she has acquired, together with her resolve to set their abandonment as a goal and to make up for what has been lost as best as she can. It is abandoning the path [that leads] away from Exalted God in favor of the path bringing one close to Him. It is obtained when there sets within the heart a readiness (*isti'dād*) to receive a revelation of the lights of knowledge.

Sometimes the postures of the [bodily] limbs lift lights into the heart, just as lights from the items of knowledge of the heart go down to the limbs. This is the secret of the exaltation of the souls by means of bodily forms of worship. The spirit of worship is devotion (*ikhlāṣ*) and the presence of the heart.[2] The bodily forms of worship follow the pattern of the capital that is the basis of trade. Following upon that, the supererogatory prayers are like the profit by means of which one achieves success in the gradations.[3] One must perform the necessary [religious] obligations and, barring any impediment, whatever one can of the supererogatory prayers.

In both of them the intention and the act complete [162] the worship; however, intention is the better of the two parts, because it is the course of the spirit, whereas the act is the course of the body. Intention is the heart's inclination towards the good; try to get plenty of it! The reward for the act is a function of the intention. Sleeping with the intention of restoring briskness in the doing of good is better than worship in a state of fatigue.[4]

Love of this world is the chief offense, repelling as it does freedom and abstention from it [this world].[5] Abstention is refraining from engagement in the pleasures of the body and its faculties unless it be out of consideration of absolute necessity. It increases one's contentedness in that one abandons many habitual tasks.[6]

For "those who can see," this world is naught, since this world is limited, whereas the next world has no limit.[7] Whosoever is disposed to abstain from it and incline away from it may possibly aggrandize it and incline towards it even as he thinks himself to be inclining away from it. For this reason, the abstention of the "true inquirers" consists in despising it, whereas the abstention of others is some praxis by means of which they try to get plenty of it in the next world; I mean, the sensual delights that are very despicable relative to the spiritual delights, as you know.[8]

The soul is one; so when she is engaged in something, she is deterred from its opposite. For this reason, this world and the next have been compared to two adversaries: when you have pleased one of them, you have angered the other.

Contemplating just how little this world is useful and how intense its misery is, as well as the speed with which it disappears, is among the things that facilitate abstention from it. Whatever does not remain after death belongs to this world. It was created only so that one may use it to equip himself for the next world. Whoever minimizes his involvement in it to only so much as is indispensable is saved. Whoever engages in its pleasures, forgetting for what purpose it exists, is lost! Whoever thinks that he will be on intimate terms with it with his body, but will keep it out of his heart, is fooling himself.

Insulating oneself from people and getting rid of any ambitions in their direction has sundry benefits; but so also does mingling with them. One decides in favor of one of the two options according to the person and the situation. Nonetheless, friendship and fraternity should be with God alone, not with this world. Insulating oneself from the world is more useful. However, the ignorant must socialize for purposes of instruction. Moreover, the initiates' occupation with constant remembrance (*al-dhikr al-dā'im*), [163] abandoning sensation and movements, and disengaging from thoughts that drag one into the world, will doubtless help them to achieve their goal.

One must be on the watch for Satan's machinations, which take different forms. Among his machinations [is this]: he calls to the good but intends for the bad, as when he beckons to a good act (*mafḍūl*) in order to keep one away from an even better one (*al-fāḍil*), or when he calls upon a person to the good so as to drag him into a great sin, such that the good will not be sufficient to redeem the bad. For example, how many people have become infuriated for causes other than God, thinking that they are angry for God![9]

There are many forces [at work] in the one body, and they are in the care and custody of the soul. Just how the soul manages these forces, exerts control over them, and takes care not to be deceived by the seductive talk of some of them is a difficult matter which is easy only for those who have learned about the cure for the ills of the soul and its notions (*khawāṭir*). "Notion" (*khāṭir*) refers to those thoughts reverberating in the soul that beckon toward a certain thing, being joined to either a supernal or lower sensation. Among the satanic perils are unfettered imagination (*wahm*), which is the imagination's contradicting the intellect regarding things that are not susceptible to sensation; for example, its denial of an existent that does not lie in any direction.[10] Make an effort to distinguish between the good notion and the bad!

Chapter Two

On fear of God and guarding the exterior limbs

You must restrain the soul, reining her in by means of the fear of God, which consists in emptying the heart of sins. Avoiding prohibitions is harder for people than carrying out positive commandments. You should demand this of your limbs and faculties, which constitute God's bounty upon you; be careful not to utilize His bounty to sin against Him! Do not look with your eye upon something forbidden, nor upon any of God's creation [164] with scorn.

Should you see a sinner, say to yourself: maybe his inner conscience (*sarīra*) is completely with God, and that will wipe away his sins; he will surpass all the acts of worship that I have performed. Do not set your ear to slander and indecency; [do not] immerse yourself in vanity or mention people's misdeeds.

Keep your tongue from lying, even in jest; for speech is one of the things that ennoble humans, [setting them] apart from other animals. Speech was intended only so that a person may know what is in his friend's soul; but lies turn this goal around, with the result that he [the liar] is baser than the dumb animals. If you want to know just how disgusting lying is, look at how you are repelled by the liar; so be disgusted with yourself, just as you would be disgusted with someone else.

Don't break a promise, and take care to fulfill a commitment. Don't say anything that would offend someone were he to hear it, neither bluntly nor by way of hint. Put aside quarrel, backbiting, and controversy in your discourse, even if you are right and the person you would quarrel with is wrong.

Don't consider yourself righteous and praise yourself—that's a defect with respect to your standing with people.[11] Don't curse any of God's creations, be it a person or anything else; don't come between the servants and God. There is no blame for not cursing Iblīs [Satan]—so how can there be for [not cursing] anyone else?[12] Don't call down evil upon any person; if he has wronged you, refer his case to God. Abandon derision, mockery, and much merrymaking.

Refrain from putting into your belly food or drink that is forbidden to you. Take care not to procure either forbidden or doubtful [i.e., possibly forbidden] things; be careful to procure only what is permitted. Take less than what leads to satiety, because satiety makes the bodily organs heavy and gives victory to Satan's soldiers. As for your [sexual] pleasure (*faraj*), guard it from all that God has forbidden; help yourself in this by avoiding satiety, and by neither looking at anything forbidden nor thinking about it. Keep your hands from hurting anyone with them, keep your feet from running after something forbidden or going to any wrongdoing; this is what you must watch over in what concerns your exterior limbs.

[165] Chapter Three

On protecting the heart from the scourges that are particular to it

The heart is nothing but the eye of the soul (*'ayn al-nafs*), not the well-known organ.[13] It is a king who is obeyed and a chief who is followed. All the organs constitute its retinue. If the one who is followed is sound, then the follower is sound. But if the king is ill, then so is his flock.[14] It is the storehouse of the servant's precious jewel, as well as every momentous concept, such as the intellect, knowledge of Exalted God, pure intention, the types of sciences and wisdoms, and all noble character traits. A treasure such as this deserves to be protected from filths and scourges.

One of the scourges of the heart is prolonged hope (*ṭūl al-amal*).[15] It hinders all good and obedience and attracts all bad and disruption. The intelligent person will not forget to remember death. A person must not let his moments be free from thinking about those bygone centuries and colleagues who have passed, and what each one of them enjoyed regarding honor, glory, money, and servants. He should tell himself that if he lives this evening he may not be here on the morrow, and if he does not die suddenly, his death-illness may suddenly come over him.

Envy is one of the scourges of the heart. The envious person is always defeated. How can he be victorious in his pursuit when what he seeks is that God's blessing be taken away from His servants? It is enough for envy to be deemed a bad trait in that it does more harm to the one who possesses it than it does to the person who is envied; the person who is envied may even not be harmed at all! All of humanity are God's servants and His dependents. One must love them and look after their well-being. Whoever loves them loves His dependents and servants.

[166] Haste is one of the scourges of the heart. The servant may set as a goal [to acquire] a house, and be hasty in obtaining it, though this was not at its [proper] moment.[16] Thus he became impoverished, or abandoned the effort, or was killed in the effort, which was denied. So also when he prays much, he wants to be answered quickly.

Grandeur, eminence, and pride are among the scourges. Pride is one of the attributes that belong to the Lord alone, and he [the servant] is not allowed to compete with His attribute. Its cure consists in the person's knowing his baseness relative to those who dwell in the higher world, as far as knowledge, servitude, and power are concerned.[17] He should recall that he comes from a filthy drop and that all that he has—money, beauty, retinue—are exterior to his essence and will not remain for him.[18] He has no knowledge of the moment of his demise—indeed, of most of his circumstances. The lowliest thing is beyond his capability.

He should then consider that the earth and all that lies upon it—indeed, all the elements and that which they comprise—are as nothing compared to the highest heaven. Taken relative to the angels, the human is like the lowest worm or gnat in its relation to the human. Indeed, the differential is many times greater than that.

Vanity is one of the causes of pride, but it is pure ignorance. Should a person form a high opinion of himself on some account, he should think about his dreaded departure, which is near; he should be amazed that he was given this [life] not by right, and not of his own. He should say to himself: just as this was given to me for no reason, so will it be quickly taken away without cause.

Anger is one of the difficult diseases. It is an unstable madness. It must be broken by repeated meekness together with avoiding things that anger. One must keep in mind what a bad trait it is, and how much restraining one's anger brings with it recompense and excellence. Haughtiness and vanity are among its most powerful causes; when they are broken, so is it.

[167] Stinginess is one of the diseases of the heart. Its remedy is the knowledge that money belongs to God, who consigned it to him [any human] only so that he may dispose of it for the most important religious and civil matters. Whatever is left from it should then be given over to the poor and helpless of his kind.[19] God made this mandatory for him out of justice for His servants,

bestowing mercy upon them and providential caring upon them. He [the human] ought not to be annoyed that he distributes it charitably. Instead, he ought to believe that whoever has been given something by him has, in fact, taken part of his [the recipient's] own lawful share. As for himself, he should believe that he has delivered the lawful share to the one who deserves it, and the debt to the one to whom it is owed. If getting money is for the purpose of pleasure and lusts, why then people of intelligence find [divine] recompense and a good reputation to be more pleasurable than that. But if he does it in order to leave it behind for his child, or for someone who follows in his path, then he is leaving his child or someone else the good but going to meet God with evildoing. If his child is good, then God will provide for him; but if his child is immoral, he [the giver] has helped him to sin. How many people have died poor while their child became rich, and vice versa. Whoever takes it upon himself as a duty to spend continuously will have this become for him a habit and a nature.

Love of honor is [a] more serious [defect] than love of money because attaining money by means of honor is easier than attaining honor by means of money.[20] It [honor] is one of the divine attributes, and for that reason it something that is naturally loved. The secret of this [innate love of honor] is that the spirit bears some relationship to the divine thing. For that reason, man, who is incapable of [physically] mastering the heavens, the angels, the mountains, and the seas, longs to master all of them by means of knowledge. Similarly, someone who cannot put in place the wonders [of creation] longs to know how they are arranged. Thus, when a person pictures to himself that the members of his species are enslaved to him, he then would love to have them be enslaved to him, so that he would take possession of their hearts.

For this reason, those who have lofty ambitions love to have their fame spread [168] and their command carried afar, even to lands where their feet have not passed, nor have they seen their people.[21] Now true high standing is a sign of a noble soul and is not blameworthy; what is blameworthy is to seek fanciful promotion, for that is something transitory that has no permanence.

True perfection, which consists in closeness to Exalted God, is laudable prestige. But seeking after fanciful perfection consists in the soul's stalling at the lower thing.[22] A reasonable person knows that even if all of the people on earth were to bow down to him, neither the one bowing nor the one bowed to is permanent. Everything that perishes is despicable. Any great thing that does not last forever is [really] small, and every span of time that comes to an end is short. That small amount of pride, which preserves him against wrongdoing and enmity, is sufficient for a man. To seek more than that is an unnecessary excess. A lot of it for [one] person may be a little for someone else, and vice versa.

Hypocrisy is one of the greatest scourges. It consists in seeking standing in people's hearts by means of devotion and acts of goodness.[23] Whoever intends his devotion for the servants believes that they are more capable of doing him good or harm than God is.[24] It is enough for the hypocrite [to realize] that, were people to know the hypocritical intention in his innards, they would hate him. Safety from hypocrisy is found in hiding one's devotions.[25]

You, if you have seen the scope of obeisance to Exalted God, and you have also seen the incapability of folks [to meet this demand], along with their weakness and ignorance, then you would not take them into consideration in your heart. Forsake their praise, extolling, and aggrandizement, which is of no value; don't make any of that a goal of your obeisance.

Avoid taking an oath by Exalted God even if you are in the right, unless by religious law you have recourse to that. But in that case, [169] formulate precisely what is correct and be wary of falsehood. For a false oath is one of the gravest offenses; you will not thereby acquire anything useful, nor will you ward off by it an earthly harm.[26]

A character trait is a [certain] configuration of the soul, from which action readily issues, without deliberation or constraint; constraint may in fact be a path towards the acquisition of the character trait, by means of habituation.[27] The gap between people with regard to inner goodness is no less than the gap between the goodness [seen] on the outside, but rather greater. A person may think himself to have a good character, when in fact he is devoid of it.

Chapter Four

On the stations that are required of the person seeking worship and knowledge

One of the [Sufi] stations (*maqāmāt*) that the seeker after worship and knowledge of the Truth stands in need of is reliance (*tawakkul*). It consists in constantly paying good heed to the divine decree (*al-qaḍā' wa-l-qadar*) in all events, rather than limiting one's perspective to natural causes.[28] The knower ascertains for himself that God is the Provider; there is no Agent other than Him. Indeed, he [the knower] will not see anything in reality other than

Him. Its multiplicity [Reality's apparent multiplicity] is the fault of whoever splinters his vision, like someone who sees a person limb by limb. Were he to view him as a totality, neither the thought of single [individual entities] nor the sight of multiplicity would come to his mind.

Linking causes to effects does not infringe upon the servant's true reliance on God; rather, if one adds to it faith in [divine] kindness, goodness, and wisdom, the result is firmness in reliance. Whoever ascertains for himself that God is not at all stingy towards creation; that He does not hold back anything for their good; that He delivers to them sustenance already when they are in their mothers' bellies, after which He delivers it to them when they are helpless children; that He sustains the animals, in all of their diversity, guiding them to what is good for them and towards that which [provides for] their endurance, as individuals and as species: it behooves [whoever ascertains all of the above] to entrust Him with his affairs and to trust in Him. Know, however, that the sustenance that is guaranteed [by God, *al-Razzāq*] is that which maintains the structure [of the human body], [170] not that which is more than the amount needed.

If some affair is unclear to you, and you do not know whether it is proper or not, entrust your affair to God, and it cannot but turn out for the proper and good. But if you think otherwise, or you think there to be some defect in [our this-worldly] imperfect reality, know then, from the principles that have already come [in this tract], that this evil is tied to some perfection or good that is greater than it. A compassionate parent will beat his child for his benefit, and also give him distasteful medicine to drink, apply suction cups and phlebotomize him, though the child dislikes this; perhaps he may even think that he [the parent] is seeking to harm him and not to help. God is even more merciful towards His servants than a father or a mother. How could it be otherwise, seeing that the compassion and mercy that He has implanted in the nature of the father and mother is a small portion of His own mercy and compassion?

However, reliance [upon God] does not stipulate abandoning earning [one's living] or medication, for example, because the linking of causes to effects is part of God's way of doing things (*sunnat Allāh*), and it will not change.[29] One must rather hold that the hand, the food, the seed, the capacity to take nutrition, the inspiration to make an effort as well the ability to do so—all [these] and the rest [as well] are within the power of Exalted God; they are the effects of His watching over His creatures and His wish for their well-being.[30] Trust can only be in God, who created them, not in them [God's creations]! He is capable of removing them and nullifying any benefit [that may be had] from them.

One of the virtues of entrusting [God with one's needs] is the security of the heart, which is just the same as [the way] your heart is secure from any enmity towards you on the part of someone whom you rely upon since you know his counsel and goodness. You must be content with whatever God does. Contentedness is an acquired trait (*malaka*) that gives the soul the capacity [to deal with] whatever bereaving event it may meet up with in a manner such that one is not harmed by its occurrence.[31] Instead, [one senses] a delicate enlightenment by considering the wondrous cause that led to [the event].[32] Something may be pleasing from one aspect, [171] but loathsome from another, as sin is for the person who thinks that that is decreed by God. It may thus be pleasing, insofar as it is His decree, but loathsome insofar as it makes one distant from Him.

Remain forbearing whether times are good or bad.[33] In good times, [do so] lest you overdo it and thus forget where you come from and where you are going [your end]. But as for the bad times, [do so] lest your apprehension and anxiety on account of fear prevent you from worshipping your Lord or lead you to loss of faith in mercy and providence.

The beginning of wisdom is fear of God.[34] Fear is the hurt [felt by] the soul on account of something despicable whose coming about in the future she fears. Hope is her delight in that which suits her, when she has been informed of its possible realization in what is about to happen.[35] When you recall the perfect majesty of God, His augustness, the grandeur and awe of His rule; and then the furious anger against which neither heavens nor earth can maintain itself; and then the utmost degree of your forgetfulness and your many sins, taken together with the precision of His command, the strictness of His actions, the compass of His knowledge and vision over defects and hidden things, the fury of His threat, and the pain of His punishment, such that hearts cannot bear to mention it, not to speak of encountering it: all of this leads you to fear. However, one ought not to exaggerate to the point that it leads to despair; that is to be condemned. Instead, recall at once God's many kindnesses to you, as well as His extending to you all sorts of benevolences without your deserving it or asking for it.

Remember that His mercy is profuse, and it precedes His anger; and that He is the most merciful of the merciful, compassionate to those who worship him; that He is opulent and generous; and [remember] the lavish reward and awe-inspiring generosity that He has promised. If you persevere in these remembrances, you will attain for yourself hope. And if you combine the two types of remembrances, you will rectify [both] your hope and your fear. You will be walking on the purposeful path, desisting [equally] from the two sides that are to be avoided. You will then not be done in by the heat of fear nor by the cold of hope.

It (*rajā'*, "hope") differs from wish (*tamanniyy*). For whoever [172] does not care for the land, or scatters seeds but then expects a crop, is deceived in his wish. But the hopeful person is the one who achieves [by dint of his own effort] every goal that is bound to [i.e., depends upon] his choice, and only then waits in hope for God's fulfillment, and the removal of obstacles.[36]

Whoever ascertains that mercy and goodness are directly intended, whereas evil is indirectly intended, his hope will prevail over his fear, no doubt about it.[37]

He must thank God for His great benefactions and His generous bestowals. Thanks consist in the soul's taking heed of what she has received from He who has bestowed [it] upon her, giving what is needed or warding off that which is not needed, whether either is needed for the perfection of the body or of the soul, and [finally] putting in motion the organ that tells the world [literally, "the species"] about it.[38]

Whoever knows that all benefactions come from God, and that the intermediaries are enslaved and compelled [to do as God commands], will thank only God alone.[39] But whoever believes that something other than God has any hand in the benefaction that reaches him will not give authentic praise, nor will his knowledge and thanks be complete.[40] It is like the case of someone on whom the sultan, that is, the king, has conferred [a gift]. But he [the recipient] believes that the minister's care (*'ināya*) has a share in this. Had he seen the king registering this bestowal in his bureau, he would not have turned his heart towards the bureau, or to the treasurer or the agent, since they are [all] enslaved and compelled.[41]

Thanks are incumbent only upon on those by whose agency God has brought about benevolence, such as parents and the like, and then only out of pure, religiously prescribed devotion, not because the benevolence came from them personally.

There is no hardship that is not accompanied by many divine benefits. These include [the fact] that hardship is passing, not permanent. Moreover, it ultimately hints at the benefits to follow, which will in their wake wipe out the suffering of those [preceding events], just as the pain of bloodletting and cupping, or the bitterness of medicine, do not remain in the wake of the soul's [restored] health and the body's being out of danger. The wisdom within these secrets is something that cannot be properly divulged. For this reason, the servant [of God] must give thanks for hardship, on account of the bounty which follows upon it, just as he gives thanks for the bounty.

Given that [173] hearts are naturally disposed to love whosoever is good to them, and there is no true benefactor and patron other than God, He must be loved, no doubt about it. Moreover, perfection is loved on its own account, and all perfection, beauty, and brilliance in existence derive from God's perfection, beauty, and brilliance. Indeed, the perfection of anything else has no proportion to His perfection, for how can the finite be proportionate to the infinite? He who knows loves God alone; should he love something else, he loves it for His sake. Everything that is imputed to the beloved is itself beloved; the intensity of love is commensurate with the intensity of knowledge; but the lights of majesty are hidden by the intensity of their clarity and manifestation. Were the light by which things become visible to [shine] forever, so that darkness would not be known, then, don't you see, its [light's] existence would be denied, and one would not distinguish between it and the colors?[42] Were the lights not a veil for the omnipotence of God Most High, one would perceive at once the contrast [between light and color] that forces one to acknowledge the omnipotence and Omnipotent. By my life, that is an impossible assumption [to perceive beyond the veil of light]; given this assumption and its impossibility, there remains no one who perceives the contrast, or anyone who may perceive it.[43]

Love is the happiness [that comes with] envisaging the presence of a certain entity; ardent desire (*shawq*) is the movement towards the realization of that happiness. Every person who desires ardently (*mushtāq*) has found something but is also missing something. When he has attained it in totality, desire and searching come to an end.[44]

You, who seek [spiritual] well-being (*salāma*), increase [your] supplication! Make it your fortress, by means of which you fortify yourself against the things you fear. Have recourse to it in misfortune and straits. But should you supplicate in connection with some matter, but, the supplication notwithstanding, you meet up with harm, then be even more intent upon supplicating, and savor even more beseeching and crying. Perhaps you have earned what you receive on account of your evil deeds. Nonetheless, whatever inspired you to supplicate and made it suitable for you will certainly ameliorate your outcome.[45] Supplication makes [one] ready for an answer [to one's prayer] and for receiving [divine] kindnesses and lights, just as a sound temperament prepares [material objects] to receive one of the [physical] powers, or one of the souls to receive [174] the same from their giver.[46] Do not despond if the answer tarries, for everything has a predetermined time (*waqt muqaddar*), which it will not pass over. Perhaps there is something good in the delay or the absence of a response, but you do not know about it.

Chapter Five

On the improvement and correction (*ta'dīl*) of character traits[47]

You must improve your character traits and correct them. The blamable character traits are many, but their source goes back to that which I mentioned. It is not enough for you to purify your soul from some of the vices in order be purified from all of them, because some of them [vices] are bound to others, and some lay claim to [or "receive from"] the others. Just as external beauty is not complete with the beauty of [only] some organs, so long as all of them are not beautiful, so also is the case with internal beauty. Work towards the middle ground (*al-tawassuṭ*) between two opposite traits, and the soul will attain the configuration or the appropriate aspect over the body.[48]

For the middle ground is not opposed to the substance of the soul (*jawhar al-nafs*), nor does it tend to the direction of the body, but rather [it tends] away from its direction, because it always avoids the two extremities.[49] The median of which we are speaking is justice (*'adāla*): it is continence with respect to the lust-urge, bravery with regard to the anger-urge, and wisdom with respect to the intellect-urge. These are the foundations of moral virtues. Continence is a habitus (*malaka*) midway between immobility and profligacy. Bravery is a habitus midway between cowardice and impetuousness. Wisdom is a habitus midway between stupidity and [the talent for] swindling.

Branches of the lust-urge include contentedness and munificence. They are two virtues, each one of which embraces two vices. Branches of the anger-urge include forbearance, mildness, stoutheartedness, keeping secrets, and trust; and the opposites of these five are vices. [175] Branches of the intellect-urge include acuity, discernment, opinion that is on target, judiciousness, correctness, accomplishment, mercy, shame, great zeal, loyalty, and humility. These eleven virtues appertain particularly to wisdom in this trait; opposite to each of them is a vice.[50] But salvation does not depend upon total perfection. The absolute good is not granted to any human, except for rare cases, by God!

Therefore, it is incumbent upon each one, seeing that he cannot fully attain the ultimate in perfection for his species, to strive to incline towards a beautiful internal form. That [in turn] depends upon improvements (*muṣliḥāt*) upon the essence of the soul[51] and the manner in which she is regulated (*kayfiyyat al-siyāsat la-hā*), as well as bringing justice to bear upon her (*istiʿmāl al-ʿadl fīhā*). To be sure, the real intent in this area is that each person who works at it may benefit from it by improving (*iṣlāḥ*) the essence of his soul.[52] Still he is required to bring benefit to others from among his friends and those who come under his leadership. This said, I will presently resume a summary inquiry devoted especially to managing for the welfare of family and city. Guidance and direction come from God!

PART II.
ON PRACTICE
SECOND GATE

Synopsis and Commentary

In the introduction we observed that Bahā' al-Dīn al-Juwaynī, for whom the *Kalimāt* was written, was at best a very strict, at worst a sadistically tyrannical ruler. Isfahan was, nonetheless, a difficult assignment. We may suppose that Ibn Kammūna knew something about Bahā' al-Dīn; perhaps he even knew him personally. The advice in Chapter Two of this final section, that the ruler should not fly off in rage when meting out punishments, would certainly be apt for Bahā' al-Dīn; but that one sentence is ensconced in an essay on the behavior of the ruler, and there is no way of proving that Ibn Kammūna was hinting at a character trait peculiar to Bahā' al-Dīn. Like so many others, Bahā' al-Dīn may not have betrayed the more violent side of his nature until he was given a position of power.

There is also no way of knowing whether Ibn Kammūna had any information about the political situation in Isfahan, the religious groupings active there, their rivalries, and other possible causes of factionalism. In any case, the advice given in this section is by and large of a general nature. I have been able to trace a good deal of it to the seminal writings on government by the Islamic jurist Abū al-Ḥasan ʿAlī ibn Muḥammad ibn Ḥabīb al-Māwardī (Alboacen; 972–1058), especially his *Tashīl* (Simplification). Details will follow below, and specific references will be given in notes to the translation.

Ibn Kammūna prods the ruler to be just and fair but also firm, to have in mind the well-being of his flock, and so forth. The only inkling of sectarian issues is the advice to side with the weaker factions in order to keep the more powerful ones from seizing control, and a very strong and highly unusual demand that the ruler protect the *dhimmī*s, a term which designates non-Muslims who were tolerated, though clearly relegated to inferior status. Ibn Kammūna may well have had the Jewish community in Isfahan in mind. The Jewish community in that city was substantial; in 1166 the traveler Benjamin of Tudela estimated their numbers to be fifteen thousand.[1] I have no information about the community toward the end of the thirteenth century. In any event, Ibn Kammūna's urging on behalf of the *dhimmī*s, while grounded in some hadiths, has no counterpart in the literature of the period.

The references to the Torah in this section are also notable. The Torah, or "Tawrāt" as it appears in Arabic, is a legitimate source in an Islamic setting.[2] Nonetheless, there is a striking contrast between the two explicit references to the Torah (even though, in fact, the source is usually in later Jewish tradition rather than the Pentateuch) and the absence of any citations from the Qur'an. A few hadiths are cited, but as venerable dicta; the word *hadith* does not appear.

Chapter One of this section establishes the necessity for humans to live in social groupings. Ibn Kammūna cites Aristotle's famous adage, "Man is political by nature." (In its current avatar, the same dictum states that "man is a political animal.") However, mere groupings are not sufficient; the society must be harmonious, based on "mutual friendship and mutual aid."

The second gate opens with this statement: "A commendable way of life (*sīra*) is necessary for mutual friendship and mutual aid." *Sīra,* which I translate here "commendable way of life," literally means "way of walking" and, by extension, "way of living." It also means "biography," most especially exemplary biographies, especially of prophets, whose way of life is a model to be followed for all. Note, however, that al-Māwardī speaks of *sīra al-ra'iyya,* "the way of life of the governed, the subjects," which is the responsibility of the ruler.[3]

The secondary literature on Islamicate "mirrors for princes" seems to maintain a consensus that the genre presents a mix—call it a tension, call it a synthesis—of ancient Persian notions of kingship with Islamic ethics and religious values.[4] Perhaps the appropriation of the *sīra,* the Islamic ethic par excellence, for a political manifesto in which the *sīra* of the ruler is the decisive factor in the success of his rule belongs to this mix.

Societies that attain ideal harmony have overcome their "destinies" (*aqdār*). I believe that Ibn Kammūna has in mind here the forecasts of the astrologers, who predicted the fate of kingdoms much as they did for individuals; healthy societies are able to overcome inauspicious astral forecasts, while sick societies succumb even if great things have been predicted for them. The mention in this connection of *tajriba,* "repeated experience," which is the epistemological underpinning of astrology, supports the interpretation of *aqdār* as astral destinies. *Tajriba* is a form of pure empiricism and the epistemological basis of those branches of learning that do not enjoy the rigorous type of logical proof available in the exact sciences. It plays an important role in the defense of astrology and other occult sciences. However, it has an important presence in medicine as well, since many tried and tested remedies have no basis in science (then as now). Clearly, in the fields of history and government a person could appeal to experience in support of the conclusions he wished to draw.[5]

About a generation after Ibn Kammūna, Rashīd al-Dīn (like Ibn Kammūna a born Jew who served the Mongols, though Rashīd al-Dīn later converted to Islam) had this to say about verification in history: "It is the duty of historians to take the stories and narratives of every nation and group, however those people have recorded and reported them in their own books, and to relate and rewrite them from the well-known and current books of those nations based on accounts of the most reliable people."[6]

Chapter Two focuses on the cultivation of the ruler's character. Two principles guide Ibn Kammūna's advice. First, if he is to be able to govern a city or a state, the ruler must be able to govern himself—that is, to be in control of himself and his emotions, and be able to improve his character when necessary—and also to manage his household. The second is the saying cited by Ibn Kammūna, "The people follow the mores of their kings." In other words, the ruler must set an example of virtuous behavior which his flock will seek to emulate. This folk saying is transmitted by

Ibn Kathīr in his biography (*tarjama*) of the eighth-century ruler Caliph al-Walīd b. 'Abd al-Malik, titled *al-Bidāya wa-l-Nihāya*.[7] Al-Walīd was interested in building, so during his reign people would ask one another, "What did you build today?" His brother and successor, Sulaymān, was infatuated with women, and during his reign people would ask one another, "How many have you married?" Another ruler, 'Umar b. 'Abd al-'Azīz, by contrast, immersed himself in Qur'an recitation, prayer, and worship, and during his reign people would ask each other, "How many prayers? How much did you recite each day? What prayers did you make yesterday?" I translate *dīn* as "mores," as the context dictates; religion was (and remains) a way of life for the believers, not merely a set of rituals and restrictions.

Ibn Kammūna recommends that the ruler take advantage of the relative quiet of the nighttime to review the day's challenges and how he faced up to them. A nightly personal accounting of the day's activities is a feature of Pythagorean ethics, advocated and adopted, *inter alia,* by the eleventh-century physician, astrologer, and astronomer 'Alī ibn Riḍwān.[8]

The final paragraphs in this chapter again follow very closely the advice given by al-Māwardī. Note in particular the caution urged upon the ruler not to ignore public opinion while relying on his armed forces. Eltigani Abdulqadir Hamid has argued forcefully, against much of what had been written previously, that al-Māwardī urges the ruler to be aware of public disapproval of his immoral behavior, something which could eventually undermine his rule. In the face of massive civil disgust, the army will not be able to save him.[9]

Ibn Kammūna lists *raghba,* "desire," which invites harmony and proper obedience, as the first of four cardinal foundations of good governance. "Desire" in this context denotes an intense motivation or craving which radiates upon the individual's surroundings. The longer explication of al-Māwardī may be helpful in fleshing out Ibn Kammūna's terse phrasing. The former describes this as desire "that invites harmony and proper obedience and induces compassion and the giving of sound advice." The king must have a passion for just governance and sound administration, a passion that will be sensed by both his advisors and the general populace. E. Fagnan, who translated al-Māwardi's book into French, has the following note on this word: "L'expression arabe (li-raghba), d'un usage assez fréquent dans les textes, est ainsi entendue de nos jours et s'emploie pour indiquer qu'il y a concurrence d'amateurs. Kremer traduit 'um Geld dafür zu erhalten.'"[10] However, the context of Ibn Kammūna's passage mandates the translation I present.

Chapter Three is considerably longer than either of the two which preceded. It conveys the basics of good government (in a nondemocratic society, of course). The ruler should choose good aides and be sure that each one has been given the assignment that fits his talents; the king should keep close watch over officials and be wary of slander. It is best if the ruler looks upon his subjects as if they were his family.

The opening sentence once again closely echoes the guidelines of al-Māwardī: "The king cannot do without competent people; but there will be no competent people without patronage, nor patronage without material resources (*mādda*), nor material resources without justice." In a note to his edition of the *Tashīl,* Riḍwān al-Sayyid traces the passage (as is his wont) to the Persian *Aradashīr* (*Shāh-nāmeh,* "The Book of Kings"), where the adage appears in this form: "There can be a ruler only by means of men, and men only by means of money, and money only by means of infrastructure (*'imāra*), and infrastructure only by means of justice."[11] Franz Rosenthal has left us a very learned inquiry into the meaning(s) of *'adl* (and of *ṣadaqa,* which also figures in this chapter).[12]

Although Ibn Kammūna is relying heavily on al-Māwardī's *Tashīl,* nonetheless, some important sections of this chapter clearly relate to the particular constellation of factions under the Mongols and to Ibn Kammūna's personal status as a *dhimmī.* Thus, in urging the ruler not to display favoritism towards any particular group, he specifies that this includes not favoring the Muslim over the *dhimmī.* Commoners (*al-'āmma,* a word with a decidedly derogatory tinge to it; hence I translate it as "the rabble") may set themselves upon a group characterized by its *madhhab* (religious school of thought, in law and other matters) or religion, or else by following some individual or party. In this case, the ruler should always side with the weaker side. Ibn Kammūna insists that persecution of minority sects and faith communities by a ruler is subversive to his rule, and it is therefore incumbent upon him to put an end to it, quickly and decisively.

Political expediency is not the only reason, however, that the ruler must take action. Ibn Kammūna appeals to the ruler's fear of God: when the weak and oppressed find no human champion, they call upon the One Above, in true and sincere prayer that will not go unanswered. Note Ibn Kammūna's remark that God's answering the prayer now is in keeping with what was decreed of old. The decree is stated in the Qur'an 27:62, here in the translation of A. J. Arberry: "He who answers the constrained, when he calls unto Him, and removes the evil and appoints you to be successors in the earth. Is there a god with God? Little indeed do you remember." The same notion is expressed in the hadith relayed by Anas ibn Malik, one of the companions of the Prophet: "The Messenger of

Allah, peace and blessings be upon him, said, 'Beware of the supplication of the oppressed, even if he is an unbeliever, for there is no barrier between it and Allah.'"[13]

Ibn Kammūna adds that the call for help will be heard, especially if the call is made by a *mu'āhid,* a member of the covenant—a term that includes Jews and Christians. I cite here in full the short entry from the *Encyclopedia of Islam:* "literally, 'one who enters into a covenant or agreement (*'ahd*) with someone,' applied in mediaeval Islamic times to those 'People of the Book' who submitted to the Arab conquerors of the Middle East on condition of an *'ahd* or of *dhimma* [*q.v.*] 'protection.'"[14]

Driving the point further home, Ibn Kammūna cites a saying of "people of experience" warning the king against bringing harm upon the *dhimmīs*. Ibn Kammūna adds that his warning is not limited to the *dhimmis*, but rather extends "to every victim who has no one to help him." I have not been able to identify the source or sources of this maxim. We could also read *milk,* "possessions, wealth, goods," rather than *malik,* "king," as I have done. While this reading would go well with the second half of the maxim, it is out of context in its surroundings, which are all warnings to the king or ruler against policies that would jeopardize his rule. Interestingly enough, Ibn Kammūna expands the saying to encompass all the oppressed.[15]

Near the end of the chapter Ibn Kammūna cites this saying: "Beware of the supplication of the oppressed, even if he is a nonbeliever!" This maxim combines two hadiths, one beginning "beware the supplication of the oppressed," the other "There is no barrier before the supplication of the oppressed, even if he is a nonbeliever."[16] It is noteworthy in this connection that Ibn Kammūna makes no mention at all in the *Kalimāt* of the restrictions and demeaning ordinances that were commonly imposed on *dhimmīs* in Islamic states.[17] These may not have been in force as a result of the *yasa* (decree) issued by Chinggis Khan charging his sons not to favor one religion over the other, and thus in effect abolishing the distinction between Muslims and *dhimmīs*.[18] Nonetheless, as we have seen, certainly the *dhimmīs* remain a recognizable social group, and Ibn Kammūna must warn the new governor against oppressing them.

Chapter Four contains a strong dose of philosophy. How could someone of Ibn Kammūna's bent hold off for so long before addressing the philosophical principles underlying his political message? Justice is one way of describing the deity's manner of interacting with creation; it is manifest in the design of the human body and in all the components of the cosmos, animate and inanimate alike. The cosmos is a macro-anthropos, just as the human is a microcosm. These philosophical truisms were widespread at the time. If this is kept in mind, it will be clear that to act justly is to follow God's lead. Another saying cited by Ibn Kammūna in this connection relays that the king can survive heresy but not injustice. That is quite a statement: social justice is more important than religious orthodoxy!

The paragraph which begins, "It has been transmitted that all people are God's dependents; the more they look after their [own] dependents, the more endeared they are to Him," illustrates beautifully how Ibn Kammūna is able to draw on diverse religious traditions and weave his selections into a single, coherent ethical message. He begins by citing a hadith in a version that differs slightly from the one relayed in various collections; "All people are God's dependents; the more they look after their [own] dependents, the more endeared they are to Him." The hadith urges at the same time both the notion of "the family of man," as we are all God's children, family, or dependents (the Arabic *'iyāl* may be translated by all three) and that of *imitatio dei;* we all depend upon God, and God loves most those who look after His dependents: in other words, those who help their fellow humans. There are many variations of this hadith in the different collections, and they are generally considered weak or worse—which does not mean that they are invalid, only that the chain of transmission from the Prophet is unreliable.

Ibn Kammūna then cites, not the Torah, but a passage from the Torah whose "meaning" he conveys. It is, of course, an interpretation of the verse "Love thy neighbor" (Leviticus 19:18). In his Law Code (*Mishneh Torah,* Laws of Mourning 14:12) Maimonides writes, "All those things that you would like your friend to do for you, do for him, with regard to Torah and commandments." The precept from Leviticus appears three times in the Christian Bible and as a hadith (the thirteenth of al-Nawawī's forty exemplary hadiths, certified by both Bukhārī and Muslim, the most authoritative scholars of hadith; the Arabic text of Ibn Kammūna is not quite the same as the hadith). In saying that this imperative "embraces most of the noble traits and political good-doings," Ibn Kammūna echoes the Talmudic tradition that the message of the entire Torah is encapsulated in that one biblical verse.

Ibn Kammūna then expands the imperative to include all animals that possess sensation, presumably because they will feel pain if hurt or killed. There may be some Buddhist influence here. Especially in the eightfold path (more rigorous than the five precepts of "lay" people), Buddhists take it upon themselves not to kill or harm any living animal. Though other Indian traditions practiced nonviolence towards animals, in the thirteenth century this teaching was identified primarily with Buddhist narratives, especially from the biography of the Buddha. Indeed, the Buddha himself has been reincarnated in animals, a tradition related, *inter alia,* by Marco Polo.[19]

Ibn Kammūna stops short of banning the slaughter of animals for consumption. To be sure, Buddhists are allowed to eat meat, and in practice many do.[20] Nonetheless, Buddhism stands alone in its extreme rejection of violence towards all animals.[21] Speaking of Islam and Buddhism, Peter Jackson observes that "there was evidently some dialogue between representatives of the two faiths." Jackson adds: "Buddhists appear to have migrated into the Ilkhanate in significant numbers," and the thirteenth-century Mongol ruler Hülegü Khan and his immediate successors "placed great confidence in Buddhist priests and monks."[22]

There is some evidence that Indian attitudes towards animals made lasting inroads in the Mongol dominions in Iraq and Iran. For example, even after his conversion to Islam, the late-thirteenth-century Ilkhanate ruler Maḥmūd Ghāzān endowed shelters for birds, a practice that is associated with Buddhist and Hindu attitudes towards animals.[23] It is not clear to me just how rooted these ethics are in Islam. Richard Folz observes that "many Muslim scholars today, when asked about animal rights in Islam, are quick to assert that Islam has always been 'animal-friendly' but do not explore the issue beyond the rehearsing of some scriptural references."[24] Through his circle of correspondents and patrons, not to mention his intense interest in belief and practice, Ibn Kammūna would surely have gotten wind of some of the Buddhist ideas that were in circulation.

However, Ibn Kammūna then goes on to mention divine compensation for the pain the animals suffer when killed for their meat. This issue engaged early Muslim thinkers, and, following them, some Jews as well. The Muʿtazila (an early rationalist school of Islamic theology) taught recompense or reward for animals, as the tenth-century theologian al-Ashʿarī reports in his *Maqālāt al-Islāmiyyīn.*[25] Some early Jewish thinkers, including al-Ashʿarī's contemporary Saadya Gaon in his *Beliefs and Opinions* (III, 10), accepted this idea.[26] In his *Guide of the Perplexed* (III, 17), Maimonides intimated that Jewish thinkers who hold to this view are following the lead of the Muʿtazila.[27] The ninth-century litterateur al-Jāḥiẓ presents a vivid description of the "Garden" populated by all sorts of animal life, including insects and vermin.[28]

Almost half of Ibn Kammūna's chapter is taken up with an exhortation to be compassionate to all beings "that possess a sensory spirit." The effort that Ibn Kammūna invests in arguing for the existence of an immaterial, hence imperishable, spirit or soul in animals indicates that the issue was of some importance for him. Moreover, his insistence that opponents of the idea have no proof suggests strongly that this was a matter of controversy, and that Ibn Kammūna was participating in a lively debate. Evidence for such a debate can be found in Ibn Sīnā's *Mubāḥathāt* (Discussions), transcripts of the great sage's discussions with students and colleagues—discussions that often developed into a clash of opinions. Records of these discussions continued to be transmitted, edited, and commented upon for generations.

In his comprehensive *al-Ḥikma al-Mutaʿāliyya fī al-Asfār al-Arbaʿa* (Four Journeys in the Sublime Wisdom), Ṣadr al-Dīn al-Shīrāzī (d. 1640), better known as Mulla Ṣadra, cites at length from one such discussion in which the question, whether or not nonrational animals possess an immaterial (*mujarrada,* "abstracted from the material world") soul comes up. It seems to have arisen in the course of some tough questioning Ibn Sīnā received from students concerning his views on human self-perception, which, as we saw in the first part of our text, is a fundamental Avicennan concept that is even more pivotal to the thought of Ibn Kammūna. Mulla Ṣadra injects himself into the debate, coming down squarely in favor globally (because he adds details lacking in Ibn Kammūna, and I do not know how Ibn Kammūna would respond to them) of the position advocated by Ibn Kammūna:

> The truth is that the souls of animals perceive their own selves exactly as they are (*bi-nafsi dhāwātihā*), with a perception that is imaginary (*idrāk*^{an} *khiyāliyy*^{an}). It is not by the instrumentality of the imagination, but rather by means of its perceptive nature (*bi-huwatiyyatihā al-idrākiyya*). This entails their being abstracted (*tajarrudahā*) from their natural bodies, leaving aside the forms of the imagination [which, so I take it, will exist only when the animal soul is embodied]. We have already given the proof for the abstraction (*tajarrud*) from this world of the imaginative souls.[29]

In a thorough and painstaking study, the late and much lamented David Reisman sorted out the many and various texts and manuscripts transmitting the materials that make up the *Mubāḥathāt*.[30] However, he missed Mulla Ṣadra's citation of this debate, including this interesting introduction: "The second argument, and it is that by which the shaykh (Ibn Sīnā) made up his mind about it (*'awwala alayhā*) in the book *al-Mubāḥathāt*. He believed it to the best thing [he had to say] about this topic. But then his students raised many objections against it, to which the shaykh replied. I have seen these questions and answers scattered in a codex comprising letters (*murāsalāt*) that were exchanged between the shaykh and his students. We bring them here in order, completing them with some supplementary remarks that occurred to us."[31] In brief, though the suggestion of Buddhist influence is tempting, the ongoing debate in Avicennan and Ishrāqī circles, as well as the emphasis on proof, or lack of it, seems to me to point in the direction of the Islamic philosophical tradition.

It remains to suggest why Ibn Kammūna invested so heavily in the immateriality of the soul or spirit of animals. I have already called attention to his near obsession with the study of the soul, but that interest focuses on the human soul and her afterlife; I do not see the discussion in the paragraphs under scrutiny here to be a natural extension of that interest. Ibn Kammūna, as noted, breaks with the Avicennan tradition in his doctrine of the preexistence of the soul. Preexistence is a necessary, though not sufficient, condition for the doctrine of transmigration. Hence, if Ibn Kammūna were also to maintain the transmigration of the soul, including her inherence in the bodies of nonrational animals, there would be a connection. But did he support transmigration? Ibn Kammūna seems to have held his cards very close to his chest on this matter. Though, following al-Suhrawardī, he does criticize some arguments against transmigration, his own position on the matter is noncommittal, as Sabine Schmidtke has pointed out.[32] Ibn Kammūna, then, adheres to a policy of "semidissimulation," to use the lovely phrase of John Walbridge, maintained by al-Suhrawardī.[33] By that phrase Walbridge intends the following: though al-Suhrawardī clearly was sympathetic to the doctrine, he was wary of publicizing his belief, because transmigration was very problematic in Islamic circles, associated as it was with groups and individuals that were considered more or less heretical. Instead, al-Suhrawardī presents the doctrine without criticism, but identifies it as Indian. In any case, not every animal would have within it the soul of a human (departed or unborn). Elsewhere, Walbridge argues that al-Suhrawardī tried "to have things both ways."[34] I at least take away from Walbridge's discussion in both places the impression that al-Suhrawardī certainly leaned towards the doctrine of transmigration, although, as his later follower Quṭb al-Dīn al-Shīrāzī reports, he may have had some lingering doubts. Note also that the debate between Ibn Sīnā and his students centered upon the self-awareness of the animal, rather than transmigration.[35] Presumably, if the soul now in the animal had migrated there from an earlier term of office in a human body, then she would have to possess self-awareness, since that is the distinguishing characteristic of immortal, immaterial beings.

Ibn Kammūna lets on that even the smallest and most insignificant insects have been granted "inspiration" (*ilhām*), a near-prophetic ability to hit upon elegant solutions. Divinely inspired knowledge among lowly animals is likely to refer, *inter alia,* to the skill of bees in building honeycombs. This ability was already called "divinely inspired" by the fourth-century mathematician Pappus of Alexandria, in book five of his *Collection.*[36]

Ibn Kammūna does not advocate vegetarianism; he acknowledges that humans are allowed to kill animals for meat or to destroy those that threaten to harm them. Even so, animals should be slaughtered by the most compassionate method. He goes on to suggest that animals may be compensated in the world to come for whatever suffering they may have endured in this world on our behalf. Perhaps anticipating scorn for this remark, he counters with some strong statements that animals have an immaterial soul.

Ibn Kammūna expects his readers to be somewhat surprised that he is devoting so much energy to discussing the immaterial soul of animals, whose existence he clearly takes to be a fact. After all, we hardly, if at all, find a discussion of this in the books written by scientists. The reason for their reticence on this point, Ibn Kammūna tells us, is simply due to the speculative character of the claim. It has not been demonstrated unambiguously that animals possess such a soul, and for that reason scholars do not raise the subject.

Astronomy offers an analogy for this approach. Professional astronomers worked with a much more complex set of orbs; the count varied, but some fifty at least were needed for the full models. However, more popular cosmology spoke of nine, ten, or eleven orbs. Ibn Kammūna may be hinting here at a "principle of economy" in astronomy whereby the minimum number of devices was employed, regardless of whether this was the true configuration of the heavens or not. The twelfth-century Andalusian philosopher Ibn Rushd accused Ptolemy of adopting such a principle of economy at the expense of precision.[37] Moreover, scientifically minded thinkers of the time were aware of the fact that their astronomy accounted only for those bodies that were visible to the eye; they could not rule out the existence of stars so far away that the eye could not detect them. This thought figured in some refutations of astrology, since the "influence" of those far-off bodies could reach the earth, but their input could not be calculated.

These remarks offer an interesting revelation of how the science displayed in all but specialized treatises is tailored to the audience. Only the most solidly proven material ought to be included, even though those who are advanced in the discipline know that there is much more to be said.

The fifth and final chapter of the *Kalimāt* is relatively short. It begins with advice directed at high-level officials—men who exercise considerable jurisdiction but still have to answer to a higher authority. People in that position must deal not just with the populace in their charge but with their own superiors and, most delicately, with rivals who have more or less the same rank in the hierarchy. Again, Ibn Kammūna's advice does not go beyond generalities. To arrive at a specific plan of action the official must rely upon "good intuition and fine talent." He ends with a statement of a philosophical-religious principle which is the basis of all behavior: the ultimate perfection of the human consists in likening himself to God to the extent possible. This principle holds within "secrets whose explanation this brief cannot contain." Significantly, the Torah as well as "the greatest divine-like sages" is cited in support.

Ostensibly the "divine-like sages" are individuals who have succeeded in fully attaining the "ultimate perfection" described a few lines above, i.e., *imitatio dei.* However, the Arabic terms differ slightly and call for some elaboration. *Imitatio dei* is my choice for *al-tashabbuh bi-Allāh,* literally, "making oneself similar to God." In Sufi writings the idea is expressed somewhat more precisely in the phrase *al-takhalluq bi-akhlāq Allāh,* or some minor variant, which means "taking on the ethical traits of God." It is thus crystal clear that the human is taking on God's moral virtues but in no way becoming divine.[38] The imperative is thus much the same as the traditional Jewish one, alluded to by Ibn Kammūna when he mentions the Torah: "Since He is merciful, so you must also be merciful; since He is compassionate, so you too must be compassionate." The phrase just cited comes from the Sifré (a midrash dating to the early centuries of the Common Era), as a homily on Exodus

34:6.[39] This is easily understood as a moral imperative. Note that Ibn Kammūna states that it is an ideal to be achieved not just in the individual's inner being but in "what he shares with others." The social dimension fits well the ethical thrust—to be compassionate, merciful, kind, and giving to others.

However, the word used to denote the "divine-like" sages is *muta'allihīn,* from the root *'/l/h,* from which derives *ilāh,* "god." *Muta'allihīn* is constructed from the sixth form; it is a reflexive of the second, transitive form, meaning "to make oneself godlike," "to make oneself divine." Now the Greeks did speak of the "divine Plato," which made it into Arabic as *Aflaṭūn al-ilāhiyy.* In Greek culture, a human (even after his death) could move up the scale of being, becoming a "hero" and eventually deified; but such an idea was anathema to Muslims, and to Jews as well. There were two ways to get around the appellation "divine": to take the adjective to refer to the person's expertise in "the divine science"—that is, metaphysics—or to take it as hyperbole for someone who has attained divine-like qualities. The first explanation was adopted, *inter alia,* by al-Ghazālī, who went on to note that the Muslim *ilāhiyyūn* (metaphysicists, clearly a play on words), including the philosopher al-Farābī, retained a residue of Greek unbelief.[40] Maimonides took the second tack in his commentary to the *Mishnah Avot;* he could cite in this context the biblical *ish elohim,* "man of God."

Hermann Landolt has pointed out that al-Ghazālī defines *ta'alluh* as "the religious attitude *par excellence,* whereby man's heart and mind are 'submerged in God,'" and he suggests a passage from the Sufi writer al-Makkī that may have been al-Ghazālī's source.[41] Resemblance to the deity was a philosophical ideal in Greek philosophy, as well as in Jewish and Islamic Neoplatonism.[42] The adjective *muta'allih* was used often by Persian Ishrāqī philosophers; in using this term, Ibn Kammūna is revealing his Ishrāqī influences.[43]

The book ends with an apology for its brevity: "Were it not for a vaporous weakness in [my] vision that prevents [me] from writing very much, as well as the length of study and other impediments, I would have expanded the discourse by adding queries and delicate proofs that I have recorded elsewhere." Ibn Kammūna himself was an oculist and engaged here in professional self-diagnosis.[44] The length of study seems to refer to the time needed to consult the books he utilized for this treatise, including tracts on political philosophy and government that he did not use for other writings. Both of these conditions, as well as the "other impediments," indicate that this book was written towards the end of his life. The *Kalimāt* must have been completed before the end of 1279, because that is when Bahā' al-Dīn, for whom it was written, died.[45] Even though the *Kalimāt* was written for Bahā' al-Dīn, Ibn Kammūna clearly intended it to reach an audience beyond his patron, and hence continued to work on it even after his patron's demise. It seems likely to me, then, that Ibn Kammūna would have liked to invest even more effort into this book, but his health, and other unnamed "impediments," did not allow him to do so.

Setting Down Principles for the Welfare of a Person's Friends, Family, and Flock, Along with the Governance Particular to [Each of] Them

Chapter One

On the utility of social grouping (*ijtimā'*), the need for mutual assistance, and its rules

An exposé which is helpful for the affairs of governance has been [given] in the preceding [section]. I will now add this: the situation of the social grouping of people and their livelihood will not be orderly unless they are like a building, in which each part reinforces the other. For this reason, the ancients said, "Man is political by nature."[1] Everyone must take into consideration his folk and brothers, his neighbors and friends, [176] the people of his household, his subjects and servants. In so doing he must communicate with them, great and small; share with them money, status, and glory; be dutiful towards them and have compassion for them; be charitable towards their poor; watch over the growth of the capital of their leading individuals; protect their property (*'ayn*), meet their needs, instruct their ignorant; display an aversion to their sins, and keep their secrets without expecting any share or compensation from them.[2]

Whoever has a family must provide for them in accordance with their needs. He should make living together pleasant by being good to them and thwarting any harm from [happening to] them.[3] He should not neglect to manage their affairs, lest their living conditions be neglected. He should raise them without the use of force and be gentle to them, though not weak. He should not make light of his people, or of his servants, lest he lose the respect he commands among them and damage the benefit he derives from them.

A commendable way of life (*sīra*) is necessary for mutual friendship and mutual aid. How many a society has had neither living conditions nor [propitious astral] destinies (*aqdār*) to set aright its affairs; but their harmony and mutual aid nullified their destinies. How many a society has had a lofty destiny, but its manifest circumstances were morbid. Therefore, their [the societies'] disharmony and mutual estrangement erased their affairs and the fulfillment of their destinies. Experience (*tajriba*) has shown this to be true for kingdoms and other [forms of social grouping].

Chapter Two

On the way of life that the king and ruler must maintain in his very soul, so as to benefit from it in the affairs under his administration (*siyāsa*)

Whosoever God has entrusted with shepherding His creatures, thus making him an intermediary between Himself and His servants, must begin by first managing (*siyāsa*) himself and managing his household as well, in accordance with the rule of government, whose principles I have mentioned, along with a group of its branches.[4] After that he should set as his goal [177] to manage his flock. Whoever demands the obedience of others when he is incapable of obeying his own self expects something that is not to be expected.[5] Thus the king must be sure to distinguish between flatterers who are scheming for whatever he has and those who are sincerely offering sound advice, even if it brings out his faults. He must be dignified in his gait and in his bearing, taciturn, dependably honest in what he says and avoiding lies in all of his discourse. He should not fly off in rage when meting out most of his punishments; otherwise, he would do wrong should he not hold back, nor would he stay true to his word should he recant.[6] He should only display anger in order to spread fear, but without really being angry; and he should punish in order to educate, but not out of anger. He should not be overcome with joy to the extent that he would be considered someone whose character is weak and resolve is soft.

He should be forbearing as events take their course, not disclosing his inner mind so that his flock not think lightly of him. He should frequently consult with his experts and counselors, then apply each one of these four tools, each in its proper place: they are mercy, severity, forgiveness, and restraint.

It is said that the people follow the mores of their kings.[7] If the ruler is upright with regard to himself, so will his entourage be towards him, by imitation and in order to draw near to him. They will refrain from many base activities, such as the ignominy of acquisitions, the shame of requests, accepting bribes, and the like. He ought to compete with the worthies with regard to moral virtues without, however, causing them to begrudge him in this. In the evening, he ought to review carefully what he did during the day, because nighttime is best for composure of thought and presence of mind.

In all of his affairs he should aim to avoid overshooting or falling short of the mark. He ought to conduct himself according to the best actions that he sees in others. In all situations he ought not to neglect caution, prudence, and acting in the most circumspect fashion. He ought not to command the good unless he has already first done it himself, nor should he forbid the unseemly unless he has already abandoned it. He should not deny [someone's] due (*ḥaqq*), if that is required, nor a plea if it is upheld; he should not disengage [from his duties] for the sake of pleasure, in which case his flock would be unattended to the detriment of his kingdom. He ought to watch over those near to him just as he watches over his enemy.

[178] He ought not to neglect matters of religion and rely [instead] upon his power and his many soldiers.[8] If they [his soldiers] do not believe that he is committed to obedience [to God], they will cause him more harm than an enemy. Were they to hear of some excellent person who surpasses him, their greedy want

for his funds will strengthen, and he cannot be secure from their assault upon him. Religion is a foundation, and the king is its guard.

Beyond guarding the religion and the choice of aids, four things constitute the basis upon which just governance is built. The first is the desire that invites harmony and proper obedience.[9] The second is the fear that shuts down any conflict with obstinate and degenerate people. The third is decent and just behavior, by means of which the affairs of his flock will maintain themselves. Should the king have a distaste for justice, his flock will have a distaste for obedience. The fourth is the demand for justice, by means of which his kingship is strengthened and the economy grows.[10]

Chapter Three

On developing good assistants and the governance of the flock

The king cannot do without competent people; but there will be no competent people without patronage, or patronage without material resources (*mādda*), or material resources without justice.[11] The officials have the status of [bodily] limbs, without which the body cannot maintain itself, nor can it function unless they are healthy and sound. The king must straighten any crookedness in them, correct what has gone wrong in them, and eliminate those who have no hope of being set aright. Each person should be assigned to that for which he is naturally inclined and built. No one should be given an office of which he is not worthy, or an office below that which he deserves; but he [the king] should not promote the lowly and despicable. He should beware of placing an [administrative] burden upon someone incapable of bearing it, only because of the intercession of an advocate or the sponsorship of the harem.[12] He ought not to hope to seize [179] the wealth of his subjects, because the wealth of his subjects is like merchandise for the king. If they are reduced and concealed [in the royal treasury], so that he does not freely dispose of it, then his profit also lessens; but if they are increased and brought into the open [i.e., invested], it [profit] increases.[13]

A competitor in affairs of state among his subjects and the common people should not be treated kindly; the same holds for important religious affairs and any deceit with respect to gold and silver. The harm [caused] by all of this is greater than the benefit. The king must keep close watch over five groups: ministers, judges, military commanders, tax collectors, and those closest to him when he is alone for his food, drink, dress, and the like.

He should not make many dismissals or replacements because if each official believes that his days [in office] are short, he will work for his own well-being during his tenure; he will concern himself with bettering his tomorrow. When the king instills in himself the desire to take but little from his employees, he instills in them the desire to take from him a lot.[14] The saying goes, "Whoever fears your harm will undermine your authority (*amr*, "command")."[15] He must keep a very close watch over them. If it appears to him that they are being disloyal, he ought to win them back by means of a just appeal; by leading them [back], he will perforce do some good that will thwart others. He should not charge them with a job that lies beyond their capability. No news, great or small, concerning his subjects and the affairs of his assistants should escape him, concerning those who dwell close by or far away. For the purposes of his never-ending investigations he spreads out informants who are reliable and free of any interests of their own in that concerning which they report.

Many a time slander will bring about suspicion, to the point that someone loyal is pictured to be traitorous and the one doing good to be doing bad; it causes more harm to the person who accepts slander than to the one slandered. But when the assistants know that none of their deeds are hidden from the king, the traitor desists from his treason and the loyal advisor is even more loyal in his ministry.

He ought to take his subjects to be like his family, having their wishes in mind, improving their lives, donating to the poor and having consideration for the needs [180] of the noble. He should pay the utmost attention to the security of the roadways and remove prostitutes and criminals from the highways. This will increase their [the general populace's] incomes, and their country will flourish. In wake of this there will be great benefit for the kingdom.

He should balance what they [his subjects] owe to him and what they are entitled to. In giving out what is due, he should not give preference to the high-ranking over the low-ranking, or to the powerful over the weak, or to the elect over the commoner, or to the Muslim over the *dhimmī;* however, he must pay more attention to the one who behaves arrogantly.[16] Should he see the commoners behaving fanatically towards a [certain] group, aiming to harm them [its members] on account of a school of thought (*madhhab*), religion, or their following an individual or party, then he should side with the weaker group.[17] In that case, the powerful will not be able to seize control over them or to harm them in any way. Putting an end to the desire of the rabble to take over is mandatory! When a stop is not put to this state of affairs, it may lead to the harming of even a great king.[18] For when the weak person sees that there is no one who cares about him, and the ruler is not helping him, he then entrusts his cause completely in prayer to God, with full intention and without turning to anyone else. Then He who answers the troubled person who beseeches Him will answer him, as it is in the preexistent decree (*al-qaḍāʾ al-sābiq*); and He will take vengeance upon the person who harmed him and deserted him, especially if the victim is a member of the covenant (*muʿāhid*) and not disloyal.[19] For this reason "the possessors of experience" (*arbāb al-tajārib*) say, "Harming the *dhimma* people [leads to the removal of] the king and removes good fortune."[20] This is not limited to them, but rather [extends] to every victim who has no one to help him.

The ruler should not allow any of his subjects to take vengeance on his own, even if this be justified. That would lead to the spread of injustice and people taking things that do not belong to them. He must prevent them from [practicing] usury, gambling, and any transaction acquisition that does not bring about reciprocal benefit for both parties. Allowing them such things entails enormous harm to the well-being of society and civic cooperation. It is good for kings when the healthy are loyal and the sick beset him; it is bad for kings [181] when the sick are loyal and the healthy beset him. He ought to befriend people of knowledge, goodness, and intellect, because a person is characterized by the characteristics of the people he associates with; and the deeds of those he befriends are ascribed to him. But he must beware of making friends with hypocrites and those who label themselves with knowledge or piety, without, however, seeking by means of either the great countenance of God.

He should reward the one who does good by doing good to him, in order to inculcate doing good into the populace, so that they will want to do good to him [the ruler]. The ruler may see someone who is not, as far as he can tell, a wrongdoer and hence deserves forgiveness. Still, should he deem that that person deserves to be punished, then he should punish him, in order to set him aright or for the general well-being. But it should not be done out of anger towards him and to satisfy his [own] need for revenge.

He must be careful to be true to his word and not to betray someone who betrays him; for experience shows that the punishment of the traitor is swift. Beware of the supplication of the oppressed, even if he is a nonbeliever![21] Nor ought he to make light of minor issues, for they may lead to major ones. He ought to know that intellect and good management are more beneficial than many soldiers and money. It is for this reason that humans rule over many of the animals that are more powerful than they are with regard to [physical] strength, courage, and daring.

Chapter Four

On the utility of justice and mercy, and an explanation of the wisdom inhering in both of them

Justice is one of God's ways of acting (*sunna*) in relation to His creation; on it rest heaven and earth. Whoever has gained access to the secrets of creation knows this, as does whoever contemplates the creation of humans—their organs, spirits, humours; their sensory, natural, and vital faculties; their qualities that work against each other, along with the cooperative support that they enjoy; their good order; the way the leading [organ] [182] derives benefit from the led, and the led from the leader. The wonders of the justice that he sees will dazzle him![22] This is confirmed by the sciences of the medical doctors, even though they have no way of covering it completely. It holds true as well for creatures other than man, such as animals, plants, minerals, their kinds and individuals; and so also the elements and everything within the heavens and earth.

The cosmos has been likened to a macro-anthropos, and the human to a microcosm. The justice in this has been clarified sufficiently in the books that have been written. Should there be evil in the world, it is like an illness that besets one individual, or like the time of a pandemic. Given that godly wisdom, divine providence, and all-embracing mercy have decreed that there be more health than sickness, it is therefore incumbent upon the nation's shepherd to establish justice and abandon wrongdoing, so that justice will prevail over evil. For this reason as well, the evildoer (*al-jā'ir;* Satan) opposes God's rule, puts the lie to His message, distorts His law and diverges from Him with regard to His creatures. Therefore, it is proper for the person who seeks His mercy to make good prevail over evil, and not to let it [evil] be tolerated for long.

Accordingly, the possessors of experience (*arbāb al-tajārib*) have ruled that the king will survive heresy, but he will not survive injustice.[23] This can only be by providence on the part of the Wise and Just One, in the manner that I have explained, not otherwise.

It has been transmitted that all people are God's dependents; the more they look after their [own] dependents, the more endeared they are to Him. The Torah has something whose meaning is: choose for your friend what you would choose for yourself. That saying embraces most of the noble traits and political good-doings. Your compassion must not be limited to the human species in particular, but rather [include] all that possesses a sensory spirit. For just as the Creator's providence reaches you, so does it reach them. The religious law has permitted you to exploit some animals and to slaughter others only for purposes of nutrition or warding off some harm. You must therefore exercise compassion [183] towards them in all things: exploit them in the lightest manner, and slaughter them in the easiest [for them] method. Perhaps what has been permitted concerning them contains recompense and good-doings that knowledge cannot encompass. You will not reject this after witnessing the wonderful items of wisdom and the extraordinary inspirations that have been created in the smallest gnats from among the animals.[24]

Do not pay attention to the judgment of those who deny that they [animals] possess an immaterial (*mujarrada*) soul, for there is nothing in the sapiential sciences that indicates that. To the contrary, one finds there sayings drawn from the niche of prophecy (*mishkāt al-nubbuwa*) that necessitates the opposite, or [at least] preponderates [in its favor]. Should you find in the discourse of one of them that they [animals] do not possess an immaterial soul, you should take it to mean that [the existence] of this soul is not for him an established [fact]—not that it has been established that they do not possess it. There is a tremendous difference between the two meanings![25]

This is the customary way [of expression] for this [sort of idea] among the ancients. It is like their saying that the last orb is the ninth, insofar as they [nine] are enough. They only wanted [to say] that a tenth orb is not for them an established fact, not that its nonexistence has been established with regard to the essential issue. Many of their teachings follow this mode. Therefore, you should not deny that the souls of dumb animals are not extinguished, or that they [the animals] receive compensations after death.

Chapter Five

On the proper conduct of the rulers of former times, and other people, and that with which the book will end

Since the person entrusted with a flock has been appointed by an autonomous (*mustaqill*) ruler, or else by another official of a higher rank than he, he must maintain his confidence in him and keep his secrets.[26] He should not seek anything of him by way of a request, but rather as a favor in his service and intimacy. He should not think highly of his discharging his duty in full and flaunt it; nor ought he to reveal the faults of his superior. He should not become close with whomever he [his superior] has removed, nor ought he to distance himself from someone he has taken as a companion. He should not violate the reigning order, neither openly nor privately.[27] Occasions for arousing suspicion or jealousy should be avoided. He should neither praise nor revile someone if he has not obtained factual reports about him. He must place a strong love for him in the hearts of his flock. Should someone approach him with a sound opinion or some commendable matter, he should not make an effort to denounce it or to change the opinion of the autonomous king, or anyone else, insofar as they [the king and others] have been pleased with it, as a precaution against someone who has come to the king before him; or [as a precaution against] someone who will do as he has done with regard to something that reached him beforehand, or who will remember this against him.

These are generalities, to which appertain lengthy details. One relies upon good intuition and fine talent, for without them there is no use in what has been said. However, if both of them are present, then it is easy to derive and set forth in detail [more information] from what I have said, provided that divine (*rabbaniyya*) providence helps. The general idea (*jumlat al-amr*) is that the ultimate perfection of the human, with regard to his own being as well as to what he shares with others, is *imitatio dei* to the extent that it is possible. Included in this are secrets whose explanation this brief cannot contain. This idea has been hinted at in the Torah as well; the greatest divine-like sages have also pointed towards it.

These are the morals that I wanted to mention in accordance with what the present situation dictates. Most of it has been garnered from the discourse of predecessors, with only the smallest trifle being what I have attained by my own thinking or what has flashed in my mind. It contains wonderful inquiries that are of great benefit. Were it not for a vaporous weakness in [my] vision that prevents [me] from writing very much, as well as the length of study and other impediments, I would have expanded the discourse by adding queries and delicate proofs that I have recorded elsewhere. However, the goal here is the important beliefs and practices, nothing else. There is enough [of this] in the books that have already appeared. I admit my shortcomings and the meagerness of my wares in knowledge. I ask God for forgiveness and for well-being; that He grant all of us success to improve knowledge and practice; that He guard us against deviation and error; that He make us among those who are led along His paths, and among those who take delight in His sanction in the eternal abode. Indeed, He is gracious, noble, compassionate, and merciful.

Praise to God, Lord of the worlds; may His prayers be upon the angels who are drawn close, His prophets who are sent on missions, His pure saints, and especially upon Muhammad and his pure family.[28] I sign off for the best.

Notes

Translator's Introduction

1. For Ibn Kammūna's biography and a detailed inventory of his literary output see Reza Pourjavady and Sabine Schmidtke, *A Jewish Philosopher of Baghdad* (Leiden: Brill, 2006); more recent but shorter appraisals are Y. Tzvi Langermann, "Ibn Kammūna," *Encyclopedia of Islam,* 3rd ed., ed. Kate Fleet et al., vol. 4 (Leiden: Brill, 2017), 130–134; and Y. Tzvi Langermann, "Ibn Kammuna" (revised February 26, 2018), *The Stanford Encyclopedia of Philosophy,* ed. Edward N. Zalta, available at https://plato.stanford.edu/archives/spr2018/entries/ibn-kammuna/.

2. Pourjavady and Schmidtke, *Jewish Philosopher,* 77.

3. Y. Tzvi Langermann, "Ibn Kammūna at Aleppo," *Journal of the Royal Asiatic Society,* 3rd ser., 17 (2007): 1–19.

4. Pourjavady and Schmidtke, *Jewish Philosopher,* 10.

5. Ibid., 13.

6. There is no comprehensive biography of al-Ṭūsī, though his "spiritual autobiography" is available in English: Sayyid Jalal Badakhchani, *Naṣīr al-Dīn al-Ṭūsī, Contemplation and Action: The Spiritual Autobiography of a Muslim Scholar* (London: Tauris, 1998). For a good account of his life and works see the introductory chapters to F. Jamil

Ragep, *Naṣīr al-Dīn al-Ṭūsī's Memoir on Astronomy* (*Al-Tadhkira fī 'Ilm al-Hay'a*), 2 vols. (New York: Springer, 1993).

7. The available scholarship on this figure focuses mainly on his work in the field of logic. See., e.g., Khaled El-Rouayheb, "Post-Avicennan Logicians on the Subject Matter of Logic: Some Thirteenth- and Fourteenth-Century Discussions," *Arabic Sciences and Philosophy* 22.1 (2012): 69–90; Sabine Schmidtke, "Two Commentaries on Najm al-Dīn al-Kātibī's *al-Shamsiyya,* Copied in the Hand of David b. Joshua Maimonides (fl. ca. 1335–1410 CE)," *Law and Tradition in Classical Islamic Thought*, ed. Michael Cook, Najam Haider, Intisar Rabb, and Asma Sayeed (New York: Palgrave Macmillan, 2013), 203–226; Kamran I. Karimullah, "Unusual Syllogisms: Avicenna and Najm al-Dīn al-Kātibī on *per impossibile* Syllogisms and Implication (*luzūm*)," *Oriens* 43.1–2 (2015): 223–271.

8. Pourjavady and Schmidtke, *Jewish Philosopher,* 11 and note 57.

9. See Sabine Schmidtke and Reza Pourjavady, *Critical Remarks by al-Dīn al-Kātibī on the Kitāb al-Ma'ālim by Fakhr al-Dīn al-Rāzī Together with the Commentaries by 'Izz al-Dawla Ibn Kammūna of the Thirteenth Century* (Tehran: Iranian Institute of Philosophy and Institute of Islamic Studies and the Free University of Berlin, 2007).

10. Pourjavady and Schmidtke, *Jewish Philosopher,* 11.

11. Pourjavady and Schmidtke, in *Jewish Philosopher,* 14n72, cautiously add that Fakhr al-Dīn al-Kāshī may be the exception.

12. Ibid., 14.

13. See Reza Pourjavady and Sabine Schmidtke, "The Quṭb al-Dīn al-Shīrāzī (d. 710/1311) Codex (Ms. Mar'ashī 12868) [Studies on Quṭb al-Dīn al-Shīrāzī, II]," *Studia Iranica* 36 (2007): 279–301.

14. The only study I know of this facet of Rashīd al-Dīn's literary output is the short monograph of Josef van Ess, *Der Wesir und seine Gelehrten* (Wiesbaden: Steiner, 1981).

15. Ibid., 284.

16. Pourjavady and Schmidtke, *Jewish Philosopher,* 11. For a detailed account of the book and its place in thirteenth-century thought, see Y. Tzvi Langermann, "Ibn Kammūna and the New Wisdom of the Thirteenth Century," *Arabic Sciences and Philosophy* 15 (2005): 277–327.

17. Pourjavady and Schmidtke, *Jewish Philosopher,* 12.

18. Ibid., passim.

19. See Y. Tzvi Langermann, "*Ithbāt al-Mabda'* by Sa'd ibn Manṣūr ibn Kammūna: A Philosophically Oriented Monotheistic Ethic," in *Illuminationist Texts and Textual Studies Essays in Memory of Hossein Ziai,* ed. Ali Gheissari, Ahmed Alwishah and John Wallbridge (Leiden: Brill, 2017), 135–159.

20. For an English translation of the *Tanqīḥ* see Moshe Perlmann, *Ibn Kammūna's Examination of the Three Faiths: A Thirteenth-Century Essay in Comparative Study of Religion* (Berkeley: University of California Press, 1971).

21. These dates are all substantiated in Pourjavady and Schmidtke, *Jewish Philosopher,* in their entries for the individual books.

22. The *Tanqīḥ* certainly stimulated Muslim and Christian refutations; see Pourjavady and Schmidtke, *Jewish Philosopher,* 112–113. Nonetheless, taken in context of the often acrid polemical writings circulating at the time, I do not think that it is proper to classify it as a polemic. Muslims and Christians may understandably have been displeased with the way that Ibn Kammūna presented their faiths, but a biased report is still a far cry from vicious denunciation.

23. This paragraph is based on the introduction to Perlmann, *Ibn Kammūna's Examination;* on the conflation of Maimonides and ha-Levi, see also Y. Tzvi Langermann, "Science and the Cuzari," *SIC* (*Science in Context*) 10 (1997): 495–522.

24. Perlmann, *Ibn Kammūna's Examination,* 9.

25. George E. Lane, *Early Mongol Rule in Thirteenth-Century Iran: A Persian Renaissance* (London: Routledge, 2003), 189, citing from

'Alā' al-Dīn 'Aṭā Malik Juvaynī, *The History of the World-Conqueror,* ed. John Andrew Boyle, 2 vols. (Manchester, UK: Manchester University Press, 1958).

26. Peter Jackson, *The Mongols and the Islamic World* (New Haven: Yale University Press, 2017); see further the Synopsis and Commentary on the last section of my translation.

27. Lane, *Early Mongol Rule,* 192.

28. These reasons are displayed in his *Examination* (102), and noted in passing by Perlmann in his introduction to *Ibn Kammūna's Examination,* 9. They were highlighted by Walter J. Fischel, before Perlmann's translation was published, in a long footnote (no. 26) in his "Azerbaijan in Jewish History," *Proceedings of the American Academy for Jewish Research* 22 (1953): 1–21.

29. From the third chapter in the last section; see the Synopsis and Commentary and notes to the translation, where I refer to some hadiths that warn against mistreating the *dhimmīs* (among many who urge the opposite). As far as I can tell, Ibn Kammūna is citing (or inventing?) an adage from popular wisdom.

30. I rely upon Lane, *Early Mongol Rule,* 197–199, for the information on Bahā' al-Dīn.

I. On Knowledge, First Gate: Synopsis and Commentary

1. Ibn Kammūna, *al-Jadīd fī al-ḥikma,* ed. Ḥamīd M. Kabisi (Baghdad: Wizārat al-Awqāf, 1982), 145.

2. The passage is cited in Reza Pourjavady and Sabine Schmidtke, *A Jewish Philosopher of Baghdad* (Leiden: Brill, 2006), 94.

3. See Everett K. Rowson, *A Muslim Philosopher on the Soul and Its Fate: Al-Āmirī's Kitāb al-amad 'alā l-abad* (New Haven: American Oriental Society, 1988), 217–218.

4. See Alan Hájek, "Pascal's Wager," May 2, 1998; rev. September 1, 2017, The Stanford Encyclopedia of Philosophy Archive (Fall 2017

Edition), ed. Edward N. Zalta, at https://plato.stanford.edu/archives/fall2017/entries/pascal-wager/.

5. Edith Hamilton and Huntington Cairns, *The Collected Dialogues of Plato* (Princeton: Princeton University Press, 1961), 94; the translation is by Hugh Tredennick. The argument has been made that one can construct similar arguments in Islam and other faiths; see, e.g., Jeff Jordan, "The Many-Gods Objection and Pascal's Wager," *International Philosophical Quarterly* 31.3 (1991): 309–317. The Wikipedia entry on Pascal's wager gives some equivalents in Islamic, Indian, and Christian thought; some references to primary sources are given, but these need to be examined closely. In any event, Ibn Kammūna's take on the argument is different from all of these; see "Pascal's Wager," Wikipedia, available at https://en.wikipedia.org/wiki/Pascal%27s_Wager (accessed November 15, 2018).

6. Shlomo Pines and Tuvia Gelblum, "Al-Bīrūnī's Arabic Version of Patanjali's Yogasūtra: A Translation of His First Chapter and a Comparison with Related Sanskrit Texts," *Bulletin of the School of Oriental and African Studies* 29.2 (1966): 302–325.

7. For more detailed discussions of this term see George Hourani, "Ibn Sīnā on Necessary and Possible Existence," *Philosophical Forum* 4 (1972): 74–86; Robert Wisnovsky, *Avicenna's Metaphysics in Context* (Ithaca: Cornell University Press, 2003), chaps. 11–14; Lenn Evan Goodman, *Avicenna* (Ithaca: Cornell University Press, 2006), 49–60.

8. For a detailed discussion see Jon McGinnis, "Avicennan Infinity: A Select History of the Infinite Through Avicenna," *Philosophy* 32 (2007): 233–250, and, more generally, Patterson Brown, "Infinite Causal Regression," *Philosophical Review* 75 (1966): 510–525.

9. See McGinnis, "Avicennan Infinity," 249, top.

10. See Parviz Morewedge, *A Critical Translation-Commentary and Analysis of the Fundamental Arguments in Avicenna's "Metaphysica" in the "Dānish Nāma-i 'alā'ī"* (London: Routledge, 1976), glossary, s.v. *basīṭ*; Herbert A. Davidson, "Avicenna's Proof for the Existence of God as

a Necessary Being," in *Islamic Philosophical Theology,* ed. Parviz Morewedge (Albany: State University of New York Press, 1979), 165–187.

11. See Richard Walzer, ed. and trans., *Al-Farabi on the Perfect State* (Oxford: Clarendon Press, 1985), esp. 63–67 and the arguments that the First can have no contrary; Walzer later (338) asserts that al-Fārābī's target is Manichaean dualism.

12. *Faḍā'iḥ al-bātiniyya,* ed. Abd al-Raḥmān Badawī (Cairo, 1964), 28, 38–39; trans. Richard J. McCarthy as *The Infamies (Enormities) of the Batinites and the Virtues (Merits) of the Mustazahirites* (New York: Twayne, 1980).

13. Jari Kaukua, *Self-Awareness in Islamic Philosophy* (Cambridge: Cambridge University Press, 2015).

14. Ibid., 97n68. Ibn Kammūna's takes on the thought experiment are well analyzed by Lukas Muehlethaler in "Ibn Kammūna on the Argument of the Flying Man in Avicenna's *Ishārāt* and Suhrawardī's *Talwīḥāt,*" in *Avicenna and His Legacy,* ed. Y. Tzvi Langermann (Turnhout: Brepols, 2009), 179–203.

15. Ikhwān al-ṣafā' viewed the world's cohesion, in the manner of a macro-anthropos, to be the greatest proof for God to be drawn from creation; see Carmela Baffioni, "Ikhwân al- ṣafâ,'" The Stanford Encyclopedia of Philosophy Archive (Fall 2016 Edition), ed. Edward N. Zalta, at https://plato.stanford.edu/archives/fall2016/entries/ikhwan-al-safa/. Maimonides too views the cohesion and functioning of the cosmos as a single unit to be an important proof for God, but studiously avoids the metaphor of macro-anthropos; this is probably due to his wariness of those who would take the phrase literally (see *Guide of the Perplexed* 1.1). For a book-length study of the concept in "Sufi philosophy" see Ghāzī 'Urābī, *al-Insān al-kabīr: ḥiwārāt fī al-falsafah al-ṣūfīyah* (Damascus: Dār al-Ma'rifah, 1999).

16. Ibn Kammūna adumbrates, though with far less sophistication, the modern debate over the self; see Y. Tzvi Langermann, "*'Ilm, 'amal,*

and the Stability of the Self in a Short Treatise by Ibn Kammūna (d. 1284)," in *Die Seele im Mittelalter. Von der Substanz zum funktionalen System,* ed. Günther Mensching and Alia Mensching-Estakhr (Würzburg: Königshausen & Neumann, 2018), 117–128.

17. On *al-muṭāʿ* in al-Ghazālī's later writings see Frank Griffel, *Al-Ghazālī's Philosophical Theology* (Oxford: Oxford University Press, 2009), 255–258.

I. On Knowledge, Second Gate: Synopsis and Commentary

1. See Items 1.3.8, 1.3.9, and 1.3.10 in Reza Pourjavady and Sabine Schmidtke, *A Jewish Philosopher of Baghdad* (Leiden: Brill, 2006), 100–106.

2. Fazlur Rahman, *Avicenna's Psychology* (Oxford: Oxford University Press, 1952), 65.

3. See Mark Schiefsky, "Galen and the Tripartite Soul," in *Plato and the Divided Self,* ed. Rachel Barney, Tad Brennan, and Charles Brittain (Cambridge: Cambridge University Press, 2012), 331–349.

4. See Thérèse-Anne Druart, "The Human Soul's Individuation and Its Survival After the Body's Death: Avicenna on the Causal Relation Between Body and Soul," *Arabic Sciences and Philosophy* 10 (2000): 259–273; Peter Adamson, "Correcting Plotinus: Soul's Relationship to Body in Avicenna's Commentary on the Theology of Aristotle," *Bulletin of the Institute of Classical Studies* 47 (2004): 59–75. The argument was given again by Avicenna's pupil Bahmanyār; see Meryem Sebti, "The Ontological Link Between Body and Soul in Bahmanyār's *Kitāb al-Taḥṣīl,*" *Muslim World* 102 (2012): 525–540.

5. For Ibn Kammūna's refutation see Pourjavady and Schmidtke, *Jewish Philosopher,* 102. See further Ibn Kammūna, *Al-Jadīd fī al-ḥikma,* ed. H. M. al-Kabīsī (Baghdad: Wizārat al-Awqāf, 1403/1982), 409–412; Lukas Muehlethaler, "Ibn Kammūna (d. 683/1284):

On the Eternity of the Human Soul; The Three Treatises on the Soul and Related Text," (Ph.D. diss., Yale University, 2010), 59–64; Muehlethaler, "Revising Avicenna's Ontology of the Soul: Ibn Kammūna on the Soul's Eternity a Parte Ante," *Muslim World* 102 (2012): 597–616. Everett Rowson, in *A Muslim Philosopher on the Soul and Its Fate* (New Haven: American Oriental Society, 1988), 307, suggests that some Muʿtazilites (an early school of rationalist theology) accepted the doctrine of the soul as a harmony, to which they added their belief in bodily resurrection.

6. See Jari Kaukua, *Self-Awareness in Islamic Philosophy* (Cambridge: Cambridge University Press, 2015); Y. Tzvi Langermann, "*ʿIlm, ʿamal,* and the Stability of the Self in a Short Treatise by Ibn Kammūna (d. 1284)," in *Die Seele im Mittelalter. Von der Substanz zum funktionalen System,* ed. Günther Mensching and Alia Mensching-Estakhr (Würzburg: Königshausen & Neumann, 2018), 117–128.

7. Ibn Kammūna presents in the *Kalimāt* a very shortened form of an argument that he expands upon elsewhere; see Muehlethaler, "Revising Avicenna's Ontology of the Soul," 610.

8. See Harry Austryn Wolfson, "The Kalam Problem of Nonexistence and Saadia's Second Theory of Creation," *Jewish Quarterly Review* 36.4 (1946): 371–391; see also note 10 below.

9. On the notion of "abode" see Harry Austryn Wolfson, *Crescas' Critique of Aristotle* (Cambridge: Harvard University Press, 1929), 577, citing al-Ghazālī and al-Shahrastānī (1086–1158), a Persian historian of religions and philosopher.

10. Heidrun Eichner, "The Chapter 'On Existence and Nonexistence" of Ibn Kammūna's *al-Jadid fi l-Hikma,*" in *Avicenna and His Legacy: A Golden Age of Science and Philosophy,* ed. Y. Tzvi Langermann (Turnhout: Brepols, 2009), 143–178.

11. See Pourjavady and Schmidtke, *Jewish Philosopher,* 103–106, entry 1.3.10.

12. This is how the doctrine was presented by al-Bīrūnī in his book on India: "This migration begins from low stages, and rises to higher and better ones": Edward Sachau, trans., *Alberuni's India,* 2 vols. (London: Kegan Paul, 1910), vol. 1, p. 51.

13. See Leonard Lewisohn, ed., *The Philosophy of Ecstasy: Rumi and The Sufi Tradition* (Bloomington, Ind.: World Wisdom, 2014), 170.

14. Langermann, "*'Ilm, 'amal,* and the Stability of the Self."

15. See further Shlomo Pines, "The Arabic Recension of *Parva Naturalia* and the Philosophical Doctrine Concerning Veridical Dreams According to *al-risāla al-manāmiyya* and Other Sources," *Israel Oriental Studies* 4 (1974): 104–153, reprinted in *The Collected Works of Shlomo Pines,* vol. 2 (Jerusalem-Leiden: Magnes & Brill, 1986), 96–145; Rotraud E. Hansberger, "How Aristotle Came to Believe in God-Given Dreams: The Arabic Version of *De divinatione per somnum,*" in *Dreaming Across Boundaries: The Interpretation of Dreams in Islamic Lands,* ed. Louise Marlow (Cambridge: Harvard University Press, 2008), 50–77.

16. Y. Tzvi Langermann, *Yemenite Midrash: Philosophical Commentaries on the Torah* (New York: Harper San Francisco), 99. On Sufi training see John O. Voll and Kazuo Ohtsuka, "Sufism," in *The Oxford Encyclopedia of the Islamic World,* Oxford Islamic Studies Online, at http://www.oxfordislamicstudies.com/article/opr/t236/e0759. (accessed January 26, 2017.) Abū al-Ḥasan al-Shādhilī, a major Sufi thinker, took the training of the soul to be the essence of Sufism; see Elmer H. Douglas, *The Mystical Teachings of al-Shādhilī* (Albany: State University of New York Press, 1993), 4–6, 28.

17. For Ibn Sīnā's view see James Hankins, "Ficino, Avicenna and the Occult Powers of the Rational Soul," in *La magia nell'Europa moderna: tra antica sapienza e filosofia naturale. Atti del convegno,* ed. Fabrizio Meroi and Elisabetta Scapparone (Florence: Olschki, 2003), vol. 1, pp. 35–52; Dimitri Gutas, "Avicenna: The Metaphysics of the Rational Soul," *Muslim World* 102.3–4 (2012): 417–425.

18. See further Jorge Mittelmann, "Neoplatonic Sailors and Peripatetic Ships: Aristotle, Alexander, and Philoponus," *Journal of the History of Philosophy* 51 (2013): 545–566.

19. "Guidance" or "emanation" are two ways to describe human experiences of the same divine munificence.

20. Ibn Sīnā, *al-Shifā', Nafs,* 4.4, ed. J. Bakos (Prague: Nakladatelsví Čekoslovenské Akademie Véd , 1956), 195; see further Robert E. Hall, "The 'Wahm' in Ibn Sīnā's Psychology," in *Intellect et imagination dans la philosophie médievale,* ed. Maria Candida Pancheco and Jose Francesco Maerinhos, 3 vols. (Turnhout: Brepols, 2006), 1:533–549.

21. See Alexander Treiger, *Inspired Knowledge in Islamic Thought: al-Ghazālī's Theory of Mystical Cognition and Its Avicennian Foundation* (London: Routledge, 2012), 54–55.

22. Ibid., 48–55 and notes.

23. Ibn Sīnā, *al-Ishārāt wa-l-Tanbīhāt,* ed. Suleyman Dunya, near end of the section on Sufism, Namaṭ 8, faṣl 8 (Cairo: Dar al-Ma'arif, 1957–1960), vol. 4, p. 21.

I. On Knowledge, Second Gate: Translation

1. Though *aḥwāl* is usually translated "states," and this is the common rendering of the term in a treatise on the soul ascribed to Ibn Sīnā (concerning which see D. Gutas, *Avicenna and the Aristotelian Tradition* [Leiden: Brill, 1988], 305), the context dictates the translation I offer here, "features." See Nasir ad-Din Tusi [Naṣīr al-Dīn al-Ṭūsī], *The Nasirean Ethics,* trans. G. M. Wickens (London: George Allen and Unwin, 1964), 74: "In speculative philosophy it has been made clear that those psychical qualities which are quick to decline are called states, while those slow to decline are known as habits." States or, as I prefer to call them here, features, are transitory qualities which the soul may acquire but does not hold on to or assimilate.

2. Ibn Kammūna deals here in summary fashion with some competing medieval psychologies; see the Synopsis and Commentary.

3. The soul must simultaneously perceive, for example, the look and smell of a delicacy, conveyed to her by the senses from outside, and her own internal emotions of lust in order to decide whether to indulge in the item or decline.

4. Regarding my translation, "nor is she a state within one"—that is, within one body—I had at one point considered emending the heading to read *ḥālla,* "inhere" (from the root *ḥ.l.l.*, here an adjective), rather than *ḥāla,* "state" or "condition" (from the root *ḥ.w.l.*, here a noun), even though one would ordinarily expect a noun here. Orthographically, my emendation would mean that the *shadda* has been omitted in the manuscripts, something which is quite commonly done. The emendation would have been justified by the discussion within the chapter, in which Ibn Kammūna rejects the theory that the soul is an inherence (*ḥulūl*) within a bodily part. However, I think now that Ibn Kammūn has in mind a transient, unstable state, such as harmony. The simplicity of the soul is a problematic doctrine. Ibn Kammūna may be anticipating criticism of his position when he asserts here that there is no *external* complexity. See the Synopsis and Commentary and the discussion later on in this section.

5. These ideas of the "harmony" of the soul are rejected by Ibn Kammūna in other places as well. See the Synopsis and Commentary.

6. The stability of the individual's identity (or perhaps self-identification) over the course of a lifetime of changes is a critical issue for Ibn Kammūna; see Y. Tzvi Langermann, "*ʿIlm, ʿamal,* and the Stability of the Self in a Short Treatise by Ibn Kammūna (d. 1284)," in *Die Seele im Mittelalter. Von der Substanz zum funktionalen System,* ed. Günther Mensching and Alia Mensching-Estakhr (Würzburg: Königshausen & Neumann, 2018), 117–128.

7. A particularly difficult passage, not at all amenable to a fluid English translation. Simply put, Ibn Kammūna's point is this: Whatever the soul may be, whether it is material or not, the human is not "with her" if he is not aware of himself. Whenever the person is not aware of himself, there is a "disconnect" between the being inhabiting the body and the true, stable, imperishable self.

8. Concerning the theories that are rejected here, see Y. Tzvi Langermann, "The Soul in *Kalimāt Wajīza,* Ibn Kammūna's Statement of Abrahamic Philosophical Piety," *Nazariyat: Journal for the History of Islamic Philosophy and Sciences* 3 (2016): 23–42.

9. Literally, "connective particularization."

10. "Division into adjacent parts": literally, "connective particularization."

11. The potential or power (Arabic *qūwa* and Greek *dunamis* mean both of those things) of vision, which is located in the eye so long as the organ functions, is not the same thing as vision. Vision as such must be an essence and always *in actu;* the power of vision exercised through the eye moves back and forth between actuality and potentiality.

12. A compound and confounded statement if there ever were one. What Ibn Kammūna is saying here is this: were the simple thing able to accept "nonexistence"—a state of being (even if it is nonbeing) or an accident—then it would have to be—to exist—at the moment that it received nonexistence. The nonbeing of a compound is nothing but its disintegration into its constituent elements; but the simple must somehow receive the "accident" of nonbeing, a notion that calls to mind the kalam. See the Synopsis and Commentary.

13. According to medieval theory, the body had to maintain a certain configuration so as to be "prepared" to accept its "governor," i.e., the soul; when it can no longer maintain this configuration, due to the deterioration brought on by aging, it can no longer maintain that configuration, and bodily death ensues.

14. In their edition of the text, Reza Pourjavady and Sabine Schmidtke have chosen the reading that includes the negative particle *lā,* and I follow this in my translation. Ibn Kammūna argues all along that the soul, which is the governor and the entity that operated the body in the course of its lifetime, survives the death of the body; hence he should be claiming here that the destruction of the instrument does *not* entail the nonexistence of the one who operated it. However, the flow of the Arabic text, in particular the use of the conjunction *wa-*, rather than *fa-*, seems to show that this statement is not a conclusion but rather another step in the argument; two manuscripts omit the negative particle; see Pourjavady and Schmidtke, *A Jewish Philosopher of Baghdad* (Leiden: Brill, 2006), 155n253.

15. The compound is made up of parts. Were any single one of these parts sufficient to cause, or emanate, the simple product, then the other parts would have no effect, and we might just as well consider the simple to have emanated from the one, simple part. On the other hand, should one part of the compound not suffice to emanate the simple product, then the simple must have emanated from a compound qua compound, and then the product (the soul here) would be compound rather than simple.

16. The "form of the grouping," *ṣūrat al-ijtimāʿ*, belongs to the complex qua complex. It confers upon the set of components the status of a unified, complex entity, with properties of its own, different from those of the individual components.

17. The entity is a single simple substance; its duality consists in its possessing contingency or, in other words, in its having a cause—an attribute that does not infringe upon its inherent unity.

18. The soul's knowledge of her own essence does not add anything to her, hence she remains lower in ranking than the immaterial essence that is her direct cause. Ranking is a function of knowledge.

19. This passage is rather difficult; the author or copyist has been a bit negligent in gender agreement, which complicates the sorting out of the pronouns and their referents. Nonetheless, the thrust of the argument seems to be clear. Perfection is a function of knowledge and activated by self-knowledge; however, there is an upper limit of the capacity of beings to attain knowledge, which puts a cap on the uppermost possible placements of these entities in the ontological ladder.

20. The "very essence" can acquire perfection only directly from its efficient: that is, its direct and immediate cause. By contrast, other perfections—not appertaining to the "very essence"—can be acquired from other, necessarily secondary sources. This involved, barely penetrable discussion aims to show how the soul, and/or the person bearing her temporarily, can achieve various, necessary perfections which do not belong to the "very essence" of the self, though they may be helpful in acquiring perfections of that sort.

21. "Her causes": *fawā'iluhā;* literally, "her agents."

22. See the Synopsis and Commentary.

23. My translation follows the variant listed in Pourjavady and Schmidtke, *Jewish Philosopher,* 156n257.

24. The dissolution spoken of here is of the link between the soul and the body. It is striking that Ibn Kammūna calls the breaking of the bond between soul and body *inḥilāl,* after rejecting the notion that the soul's connection to the body is some sort of *ḥulūl* or inherence.

25. Ibn Kammūna looks to have in mind here the "well-known books" on astral governance. See the Synopsis and Commentary.

26. These paragraphs are one of several places in which Ibn Kammūna hints at transmigration, not only of the core soul but of a particular constellation of characteristics acquired in this world. See the Synopsis and Commentary.

27. The soul's life as an agent, perceiving external realities and deploying the faculties of the body in which she is located, is defective in the sense that it is not self-sufficient; these faculties require some effectuator to move them from potentiality to actuality.

28. I follow the variant reading (from two manuscripts) reported in Pourjavady and Schmidtke, *Jewish Philosopher,* 157n 287.

29. The "First Existence," *al-wujūd al-awwal,* is clearly intended to be the First Existing Being, the deity.

30. With regard to immaterial entities, proximity or distance cannot be measured in inches or centimeters; rather they are determined by the intensity of the perception. In religious terms, to be close to God is to have intense perception of His true reality. This is what Ibn Kammūna is talking about here.

31. The "Highest Excellency," *al-janāb al-aʿlā,* is another "neutral" term for the Supreme Being or deity. Two manuscripts exhibit here instead *al-ḥayā al-aʿlā,* the "Highest Life," an interesting but to my knowledge unattested cognomen.

32. The idea of *inṭibāʿ* is one of the theories of the soul's bonding to the body that Ibn Kammūna rejects; see the Synopsis and Commentary.

33. Ibn Kammūna contrasts here items of knowledge that are known exclusively by experience, *mujarrabāt,* with those verified by logical reasoning. See Y. Tzvi Langermann, "From My Notebooks: On Tajriba/Nissayon ("Experience"): Texts in Hebrew, Judeo-Arabic, and Arabic," *Aleph: Historical Studies in Science and Judaism* 14 (2014): 147–176, and the Synopsis and Commentary.

34. Here again Ibn Kammūna subtly asserts that the soul maintains the configuration she obtained in this life even after leaving the body and being reincarnated in a different one. Indeed, he shifts the burden of proof to those who deny it: they cannot tell us what removes or dissolves the configuration, the specific concatenation of character

traits, from the soul at death, hence this configuration maintains itself over the course of transmigration.

35. Once again, Ibn Kammūna looks to favor the view that transmigration, or metensomatosis, is relevant only when the soul is not purified enough to merit an eternal existence without being joined to a body.

36. The Arabic has *wa-awṣal ilā al-mudrik.* I must vocalize *mudrik,* the active particle, which is the only possible antecedent of the many masculine pronouns that follow. We shall presently see that, strictly speaking, the "perceiver" of whom Ibn Kammūna is speaking is not the person but his intellect.

37. I must emend here *la-hu* to *la-hā,* in order for the subject to be in the plural, "they."

38. This is how sense perception takes place in the medieval scheme of things; the sense encounters only the superficial envelope of objects.

39. That is, how can intellect be compared to sense, both of them perceivers, and their respective percepts; this is made clear in the following sentence.

40. This is a difficult sentence, which gave much trouble to both the copyists and the editors. I cannot be sure that I have understood it properly. First some textual matters: it seems clear enough that in the second part of the sentence, the correct vocalization is *mudrik,* "perceiver," rather than *mudrak,* "percept." The word I translated "plunging" is *khawḍan;* I select the variant listed in Pourjavady and Schmidtke, *Jewish Philosopher,* 160n324 (found in two manuscripts), but I emend the unintelligible *khawṣan* to *khawḍan.* The "excesses" would then refer to the unnecessary worries, desires, and the like that burden the lives of ordinary people. When speaking of the effect of intellect on the person's exterior, Ibn Kammūna probably has in mind the demeanor and radiance noticeable in "spiritual" people. One could

perhaps make a case for vocalizing *mudrak,* with the powerful accomplishment, stripping away of excesses, etc., all referring to the percept. However, this seems to me most unlikely, since intellectual perception is a zero sum game in which one either arrives at a true statement or one does not; there is no plunging through an exterior and interior.

41. Ibn Kammūna here employs the spiritual vocabulary of the Sufis; see the Synopsis and Commentary.

42. Necrophilia does not give full satisfaction since there is no expectation of visual response from a dead partner. I translate *ityān* as "copulation" (the word is omitted in two manuscripts, see Pourjavady and Schmidtke, *Jewish Philosopher,* 160n330) on the basis of the Hebrew cognate, *bi'ah,* which Ibn Kammūna would have known.

43. Once again, Ibn Kammūna indicates his openness to the transmigration of souls—here allowing even for the possibility for the soul's absorption into one of the celestial or terrestrial bodies, not necessarily a human body. However, he also intimates that these teachings do not belong to the "true religions."

44. It is better to be concise than long-winded in these matters.

II. On Practice, First Gate: Synopsis and Commentary

1. See, e.g., Saeko Yazaki, "Morality in Early Sufi Literature," in *The Cambridge Companion to Sufism,* ed. Lloyd Ridgeon (Cambridge: Cambridge University Press, 2014), 83.

2. Al-Ghazālī, *al-Arba'īn fī Uṣūl al-Dīn,* ed. A. Urwānī (Damascus: Dār al-qalam, 2003), part 4, p. 191.

3. My translation is from the edition of Rabbi Yosef Qafih: Baḥya Ibn Paquda, *Sefer Torat Hovot ha-Levavot* (Jerusalem, 1973), 39; see further Diana Lobel, *A Jewish-Sufi Dialogue: Philosophy and Mysticism in Bahya ibn Paquda* (Philadelphia: University of Pennsylvania Press, 2006).

4. There is now a considerable body of literature on Jewish engagement with Sufism. The following three items will provide a good introduction and further bibliography: Diana Lobel, *Between Mysticism and Philosophy: Sufi Language of Religious Experience in Judah Ha-Levi's Kuzari* (Albany: State University of New York Press, 2000); Paul B. Fenton, "Judaism and Sufism," in *The Cambridge Companion to Medieval Jewish Philosophy*, ed. Daniel H. Frank and Oliver Leaman (Cambridge: Cambridge University Press, 2003): 201; Elisha Russ-Fishbane, *Judaism, Sufism, and the Pietists of Medieval Egypt: A Study of Abraham Maimonides and His Times* (Oxford: Oxford University Press, 2015).

5. See Marion Holmes Katz, *Prayer in Islamic Thought and Practice* (Cambridge: Cambridge University Press, 2013), 103–104; see also John O'Kane and Bernd Radtke, *The Concept of Sainthood in Early Islamic Mysticism: Two Works by Al-Ḥākim al-Tirmidhī, An Annotated Translation with Introduction* (London: Routledge, 2013), 80–81n4.

6. Galen is quoted in connection with people raising their hands in prayer and other bodily movements as well, in Aḥmad b. Muḥammad al-Ṭabarī, *al-Muʿallajāt al-Buqrāṭiyya,* I, 30, MS Munich arab. 810, f. 29v. See also Shlomo Pines and Tuvia Gelblum, "Al-Bīrūnī's Arabic Version of Patanjali's Yogasūtra: A Translation of His First Chapter and a Comparison with Related Sanskrit Texts," *Bulletin of the School of Oriental and African Studies* 29.2 (1966): 302–325, at 319, question 11. Prayer gestures have been the subject of much research; see, e.g., Maurizio Mottelese's book-length study, *Bodily Rituals in Jewish Mysticism: The Intensification of Cultic Hand Gestures by Medieval Kabbalists* (Los Angeles: Cherub Press, 2016); and more generally, Betty J. Bäuml and Franz H. Bäuml, *A Dictionary of Gestures* (Metuchen, N.J.: Scarecrow Press, 1975), 120–196, for a detailed investigation into the use of hands. However, research to date has hardly touched upon bodily gestures in the Islamic context beyond recording the standard practices of prostration and other gestures ensconced in law and custom.

7. Cf. Jari Kaukua and Taneli Kukkonen, "Sense-Perception and Self-Awareness: Before and After Avicenna," in *Consciousness: From Perception to Reflection in the History of Philosophy*, ed. Sara Heinämaa, Vili Lähteenmäki, and Pauliina Remes (Dordrecht: Springer, 2007), 95–119, at 115, in connection with the views of Fakhr al-Dīn al-Rāzī.

8. The precise references are given in notes to my translation.

9. My translation is from A. Badawi, *Plotinus apud Arabes*, 3rd ed. (Kuwait: Wakālat al-Maṭbūʿāt, 1977), 33. On the *Theology of Aristotle* see Peter Adamson, *The Arabic Plotinus: A Philosophical Study of the "Theology of Aristotle"* (London: Duckworth, 2002).

10. Herman F. Janssens, "Bar Hebraeus' Book of the Pupils of the Eye," *American Journal of Semitic Languages and Literatures* 47 (1930): 26–49, at 26.

11. Al-Ghazālī, *al-Arbaʿīn*, 244.

12. Ibid., 144

13. *Kitāb dhimm al-Jāh wa-l-Riyā'* (Book 8 of *rubʿ al-muhlikāt*), III, 257 ff.

14. Cf. Frank Griffel, *Al-Ghazālī's Philosophical Theology* (Oxford: Oxford University Press, 2009), 200, in which he notes that al-Ghazālī replaces Ibn Sīnā's *ʿaql*, "intellect," with *rūḥ* in order to make his discourse more familiar to religious scholars.

15. Majid Fakhry, "Justice in Islamic Philosophical Ethics: Miskawayh's Mediating Contribution," *Journal of Religious Ethics* 3 (1975): 243–254, at 247.

16. See Tzvi Langermann, "Maimonides on the Possibilities of Moral Improvement," posted on YouTube on October 18, 2018, and available at https://www.youtube.com/watch?v=DvlZGdx-RFg.

17. Al-Ghazālī, *al-Arbaʿīn*, 238, top of the page.

18. Reza Pourjavady and Sabine Schmidtke, *A Jewish Philosopher of Baghdad* (Leiden: Brill, 2006), 170n493; al-Ghazālī, *al-Arabʿīn*, 260.

19. Ignaz Goldziher, *Die Richtungen der islamischen Koranauslegung* (Leiden: Brill, 1920), 210–213; Robert Wisnovsky, "One Aspect of the Akbarian Turn in Shi'i Theology," in *Sufism and Theology,* ed. Ayman Shihadeh (Edinburgh: Edinburgh University Press, 2007), 49–62.

20. Binyamin Abrahamov, *Divine Love in Islamic Mysticism* (London: Routledge-Curzon, 2003).

21. William Gairdner, *Al-Ghazzālī's Mishkat Al-anwar: The Niche for Lights* (London: Royal Asiatic Society, 1924), 117.

22. See Zahra Abdollah, "Color in Islamic Theosophy," *Journal of Islamic Philosophy* 7 (2011): 35–51.

23. Pourjavady and Schmidtke, *Jewish Philosopher,* 129.

24. See Mark LeBar and Michael Slote, "Justice as a Virtue," in The Stanford Encyclopedia of Philosophy Archive (Spring 2016 Edition), ed. Edward N. Zalta, at http://plato.stanford.edu/archives/spr2016/entries/justice-virtue/.

25. Herbert A. Davidson, "Maimonides' *Shemonah Peraqim* and Alfarabi's *Fuṣūl Al-Madanī,*" *Proceedings of the American Academy of Jewish Research* 31 (1963): 33–50.

II. On Practice, First Gate: Translation

1. This sentence is taken verbatim from al-Ghazālī, *al-Arbaʿīn fī Uṣūl al-Dīn,* ed. A. Urwānī (Damascus: Dār al-qalam, 2003), 191; see the Synopsis and Commentary. The "voyagers" are clearly spiritual wayfarers or spiritual aspirants.

2. This is one of many sentences that appear verbatim in Ibn Kammūna's shorter *Ithbāt* (see my Introduction); see Reza Pourjavady and Sabine Schmidtke, *A Jewish Philosopher of Baghdad* (Leiden: Brill, 2006), 190, l. 3.

3. In other words, one moves up in the ranks of the pious.

4. Even sleep is an act of devotion if it is done with the intent of restoring one's energy—energy that will be expended on worship. See Maimonides, *Mishneh Torah, Laws of Ethical Behavior* (*Hilkhot De'ot*), 3:3.

5. "Love of this world . . ." is a hadith cited several times by al-Ghazālī in the ethical sections of his *Iḥyā'* (*Kitāb Riyāḍ al-Nafs wa-l-Akhlāq*). Al-Albānī, who classifies it as weak, surveys its reception among scholars of hadith in his *Silsilat al-ḍa'īfa wa-l-mawḍū'a*, vol. 3 (Riyāḍ: Maktabat al-Ma'ārif, 1988), 370–371, hadith 1226.

6. As one learns to be content with fewer bodily pleasures, one also frees oneself from habitual tasks that were done to secure such pleasures but are now unnecessary. As a result, one becomes more content with one's life.

7. "Those who can see," *dhawī al-baṣā'ir*, those who are not blind to the realities hidden by the illusions and delusions of the material world; William Chittick nicely distinguishes *baṣīra*, "insight," from *baṣar*, the bodily sense of vision, in *The Sufi Path to Knowledge* (Albany: State University of New York, 2010),89; see also Hava Lazarus-Yaffe, *Studies in Al-Ghazzali* (Jerusalem: Magnes, 1975), 295 and notes.

8. Here Ibn Kammūna mocks those who practice, or perhaps feign, some form of asceticism only in the hope of being rewarded for this piety by sensual delights in the afterlife.

9. People delude themselves into thinking that their anger is "righteous," when in fact it is anything but that—this delusion is Satan's doing.

10. Pourjavady and Schmidtke, in *Jewish Philosopher*, note that this passage is taken from two Sufi writings of al-Suhrawardī, *Kalimāt al-taṣawwuf* and *Maqāmāt al-ṣūfiyya* (163n373). I should add that the example is drawn from a notion that is joined to a supernal sensation—in other words, a misleading thought that damages belief, rather than a lower sensation, which would refer to a bodily urge. The

misleading thought is that there cannot be an existent that does lie in any direction; this is one of the notional obstacles to accepting the existence of an absolutely immaterial entity.

11. The defect consists in the fact that you praise yourself, rather than letting others praise you.

12. Pourjavady and Schmidtke, *Jewish Philosopher* (26 and note 116), note correctly that this passage exemplifies "some pieces of moral advice that which he [Ibn Kammūna] seems to have paraphrased from al-Ghazālī's *Iḥyā' 'Ulūm al-Dīn.*" See *Iḥyā' 'Ulūm al-Dīn* (*Kitāb Āfāt al-Lisān*) (Beirut: Dār al-Qalam, n.d.), vol. 3, bottom of 118, where al-Ghazālī admonishes, "In general, it is dangerous to curse people, and therefore it should be avoided; and there is no danger in desisting from cursing Iblis, for example, all the more so someone else."

13. Concerning *'ayn al-nafs* see the Synopsis and Commentary.

14. Similar notions, though in different languages, can be found in some Islamic traditions. See, for example, al-Ghazālī's *Iḥyā'* (*Kitāb Sharḥ 'Ajā'ib al-Qalb*), cited here from *The Marvels of the Heart,* trans. W. J. Shelli (Louisville: Fons Vitae, 2010), 27: "And the heart is his king. If the king enjoys good health, so also do his armies."

15. See the Synopsis and Commentary.

16. The Arabic has *bi-waqtihi,* literally, "at the moment." I believe that Ibn Kammūna has in mind astrally propitious moments for carrying out business transactions. See the end of Chapter Four in this section for a statement that everything has a predetermined time.

17. To be a servant of God is a virtue, and the more noble the entity, the greater its servitude to the divine. Though we strive to be true servants of the Lord, we should know that there are entities whose servitude is perforce greater than ours. Just as the most knowledgeable human must recognize entities that have access to realms of knowledge no human can reach, so also the servitude of even those who

humbly submit to God is low-grade compared to the servitude of angels, for example.

18. Ibn Kammūna is drawing here upon his Jewish sources. The first passage in chapter three of *Avot,* the Mishnaic treatise generally known in English as "Ethics of the Fathers," advises us to recall that we come from a filthy drop (of sperm); if we are constantly aware of this, we will not sin.

19. Literally, "from the sons of his species."

20. This passage on honor (*jāh*) is based on writings by al-Ghazālī; for the details of the relationship, see the Synopsis and Commentary.

21. The Arabic phrase, *arbāb al-himam al-ʿaliyya,* may be a circumlocution, with the intended reference here to the Mongol leadership. Hence it is both a jibe and an attempt at an explanation for the leaders' ambitions.

22. Contrast *amr* here, *al-amr al-adwan,* with *al-amr al-ilāhī,* "the divine thing," above.

23. This is precisely the definition given in al-Ghazalī, *al-Arbaʿīn,* 168.

24. This is another criticism of hypocritical histrionics while performing prayer and other devotions; these actions are directed towards "the servants"—a common Muslim appellation for the people, as we are all God's servants—rather than towards God.

25. Sufi manuals urge worshippers not to perform devotions ostentatiously; this is the practice of those who wish to make an impression upon the multitudes.

26. This warning against unnecessary or false oaths is not found in al-Ghazālī; it is, however, a major theme of the biblical book of Ecclesiastes.

27. Naṣīr al-Dīn al-Ṭūsī opens the second division of the first discourse on his *Ethics* with a similar pronouncement: "Disposition is a habit of the soul, necessarily effecting the easy procession of an action

therefrom, without need of any reflection or deliberation": Nasir ad-Din Tusi, *The Nasirean Ethics,* trans. G. M. Wickens (London: George Allen, 1964), 74. For further discussion on the "*hay'a* of the soul," see the Synopsis and Commentary.

28. This definition is found word for word in al-Suhrawardī's *Kalimāt al-taṣawwuf,* as noted in Pourjavady and Schmidtke, *Jewish Philosopher,* 169n473. Nonetheless, the discussion continues to follow al-Ghazālī's ethics (see the next note), summarizing his discourse with occasional subtle alterations: for example, the kalam-like statement that one should recognize no "agent" other than God and the partial retraction found later.

29. This passage is found almost word for word in al-Ghazālī, *al-Arba'īn,* top of 243.

30. In translating "the seed" I follow the variant listed in Pourjavady and Schmidtke, *Jewish Philosopher,* 170n488. Much of this paragraph is found in Ibn Kammūna's *Ithbāt,* either word for word or in summary form.

31. "Fleeting," rather than "bereaving" event, according to the variant listed in Pourjavady and Schmidtke, *Jewish Philosopher,* 170n492.

32. That is to say, one is enlightened by contemplating the wondrous cause that preceded the event just described; see the Synopsis and Commentary on Ibn Kammūna's notion of contentedness.

33. A more literal translation would be: "Cling to forbearance in both the situations, happiness and sadness." *Ṣabr,* "forbearance," is a cardinal virtue—perhaps the cardinal virtue—of Islamic ethics, by no means the exclusive domain of the Sufis or of the philosophers.

34. The verse is from Proverbs 9:10. Some Islamic sources, e.g., al-Tha'ālabī, *Tafsīr,* part 4 (Beirut, 1997), 388, identify this verse as the opening passage (*fātiḥa*) of *al-Zubūr,* the Arabic name for Psalms; *khashiyya* rather than *khawf* is used to denote "fear." It is also a hadith transmitted by Abu Hurayra. The definition of fear which

follows is found, in almost the identical formulation, in al-Ghazālī, *al-Arbaʿīn,* 199.

35. The definition, as pointed out in Pourjavady and Schmidtke, *Jewish Philosopher,* 171n502, is taken from al-Suhrawardī's Sufi writings.

36. This distinction between the two concepts in its entirety, including the examples and the exhortation, are taken directly from al-Ghazālī, *al-Arbaʿīn,* 202.

37. This fairly standard explanation for theodicy asserts that all the good is an intentional product of the deity, whereas those things that seem to be bad are only accidental byproducts and not intended in and of themselves.

38. Here too Pourjavady and Schmidtke, *Jewish Philosopher,* 172 n512, find the source of the definition in al-Suhrawardī.

39. Ibn Kammūna has rephrased the remark of al-Ghazālī in *al-Arbaʿīn,* 219, explaining that knowledge is the first principle that leads to giving thanks.

40. What I translate "has any hand in" is literally "entry," "point of entry."

41. This simile is taken from al-Ghazālī, *al-Arbaʿīn,* 220.

42. The denial that light exists at all is one of the doctrines refuted by al-Ghazālī in his *Mishkāt al-Anwār;* see the Synopsis and Commentary for fuller analysis.

43. This difficult passage is scrutinized in the Synopsis and Commentary.

44. Pourjavady and Schmidtke, *Jewish Philosopher,* 173n531, identify the source of these definitions in al-Suhrawardī's Sufi writings, *Kalimāt al-taṣawwuf* and *Maqāmāt.*

45. The motivation to pray is in itself a good sign that the person is on the way to better things.

46. The Arabic has *wāhibihi,* an obvious reference to the Avicennan concept, *wāhib al-ṣuwar,* "the giver of forms."

47. The Arabic has *ta'dīl*. I translate the term "correction," as it is used in astronomy. This seems appropriate here as well. In context here, the word means bringing things back into their proper state.

48. If we accept the variant (see Pourjavady and Schmidtke, *Jewish Philosopher*, 174n544) that omits *al-jiha*, the sentence reads: "will attain the configuration and mastery."

49. Ibn Kammūna does not speak of "the substance of the soul" in the second gate of the first part of this treatise, which is devoted entirely to the soul. Instead he speaks of *nafs* and *dhāt al-nafs*. We have already observed that when Ibn Kammūna writes on ethics he is not always compunctious about his technical vocabulary.

50. Pourjavady and Schmidtke, *Jewish Philosopher*, 175n552, find the source of these eleven intellectual virtues in al-Suhrawardī's Sufi writings, *Kalimāt al-taṣawwuf* and *Maqāmāt*.

51. The Arabic has *dhāt al-nafs;* Ibn Kammūna here indicates that even this immortal entity can be molded during a course of occupancy of a human body.

52. Variants noted by Pourjavady and Schmidtke, *Jewish Philosopher*, 175n557, add "alone."

II. On Practice, Second Gate: Synopsis and Commentary

1. "Isfahan xviii: Jewish Community," *Encyclopaedia Iranica*, first published December 15, 2007, updated April 5, 2012, in http://www.iranicaonline.org/articles/isfahan-xviii-jewish-community.

2. See Hava Lazarus-Yafeh, "Tawrāt," in *Encyclopaedia of Islam, Second Edition*, ed. P. Bearman, Th. Bianquis, C. E. Bosworth, E. van Donzel, and W. P. Heinrichs, at http://dx.doi.org/10.1163/1573-3912_islam_COM_1203 (accessed March 28, 2018).

3. Abū al-Ḥasan 'Alī ibn Muḥammad ibn Ḥabīb al-Māwardī, *Tashīl al-Naẓar wa-Ta'jīl al-Ẓafar*, ed. Riḍwān al-Sayyid (Beirut: Dar al-Nahdah al-Arabiyyah, 1981), 275.

4. For a recent critical review of the genre, see Regula Forster and Neguin Yavari, eds., *Global Medieval: Mirrors for Princes Reconsidered* (Cambridge: Harvard University Press, 2016).

5. See Y. Tzvi Langermann, "From My Notebooks: On *Tajriba/Nissayon* ("Experience"): Texts in Hebrew, Judeo-Arabic, and Arabic," *Aleph: Historical Studies in Science and Judaism* 14 (2014): 147–176.

6. Roxann Prazniak, "Ilkhanid Buddhism: Traces of a Passage in Eurasian History," *Comparative Studies in Society and History* 56 (2014): 650–680, at 670.

7. Ibn Kathīr, *al-Bidāya wa-l-nihāya,* 16 vols. (Cairo: Maṭbaʿat al-Saʿādāt, 1351/1932), vol. 9, p. 165.

8. For the Pythagorean text see lines 40–44 of the poem in Johann C. Thom, *The Pythagorean Golden Verses: Translation and Commentary* (Leiden: Brill, 1995), 153, advocated and adopted *inter alia* by 'Alī ibn Riḍwān, for which see Y. Tzvi Langermann, "One Ethic for Three Faiths," in *Monotheism and Ethics: Historical and Contemporary Intersections Between Judaism, Christianity, and Islam,* ed. Y. Tzvi Langermann (Leiden: Brill, 2011), 197–218, at 153.

9. Eltigani Abdulqadir Hamid, "Al-Mawardī's Theory of State—Some Ignored Dimensions," *American Journal of Islamic Social Sciences* 18.4 (2001): 1–18.

10. al-Māwardī, *Tashīl,* 275; E. Fagnon, *Les Statuts gouvernementaux* (Algiers: Adolph Jourdan, 1915), 396n7. The note states that the phrase *li-raghba,* used frequently in the texts, is still current in our day, where it is used to indicate a competition between those with a penchant for something; Kremer's German rendition means something like "to get money for it." Clearly, the term was used to indicate negative traits of character, but, as I noted, in the *Tashīl* its meaning is positive.

11. al-Māwardī, *Tashīl,* 280. Many other references to the adage are also given there.

12. Franz Rosenthal, "Political Justice and the Just Ruler," *Israel Oriental Studies* 10 (1980): 92–105.

13. My translation is from the collection of al-Albānī, *Ṣaḥīḥ al-Targhīb wa-l-Tarhīb,* part 2 (Riyāḍ: Maktabat al-Maʻārif, 2000), 535, hadith 2231.

14. *Encyclopaedia of Islam,* Bar Ilan University, July 2, 2015, available at http://referenceworks.brillonline.com.proxy1.athensams.net/entries/encyclopaedia-of-islam-2/muahid-DUM_3909.

15. Some hadiths warn against harming the *dhimmī* (among very many that urge the opposite). However, their wording is entirely different from the saying cited by Ibn Kammūna, for example, the hadith cited by al-Albānī, *Ṣaḥīḥ al-Targhīb wa-l-Tarhīb,* hadith 5314, "Whosoever harms a *dhimmī,* I (*scilicet,* Allāh) will contend with him on the Day of Judgment." See further Ignaz Goldziher, *Introduction to Islamic Theology and Law,* trans. Andras and Ruth Hamori (Princeton: Princeton University Press, 1981), 34–36, who states that oppression of the *dhimmī* was considered to be "sinful excess," but acknowledges in a very long note that fanaticism came to bear in some traditions ascribed to the Prophet, adding, "Every attitude of mind found expression in Prophetic sayings made to order."

16. The hadith is validated by al-Albānī, *Silsilat al-ḍaʻīfa wa-l-mawḍūʻa,* vol. 2 (Riyāḍ: Maktabat al-Maʻārif, 1988), 395, hadith 767.

17. See Wadi Zaidan Haddad, "*Ahl al-dhimma* in an Islamic State: The Teaching of Abū al-Ḥasan al-Māwardī's *al-Ahkām al-Sultāniyya,*" *Islam and Christian-Muslim Relations* 7 (1996): 169–180, at 174, for two lists of such ordinances taken from *al-Ahkām al-Sultāniyya* of al-Māwardī; on the tremendous authority of that book in such matters, see 179n3.

18. See Peter Jackson, *The Mongols and the Islamic World, from Conquest to Conversion* (New Haven: Yale University Press, 2017), 299–300.

19. See Prazniak, "Ilkhanid Buddhism," 678–679.

20. See David Seyfort Ruegg, "Ahimsa and Vegetarianism in the History of Buddhism," in *Buddhist Studies in Honour of Walpola*

Rahula, ed. S. Balasooriya et al. (London: Gordon Fraser, and Sri Lanka: Vimamsa, 1980), 234–241; James J. Stewart, "The Question of Vegetarianism and Diet in Pāli Buddhism," *Journal of Buddhist Ethics* 17 (2010): 99–140.

21. James J. Stewart, in "Violence and Nonviolence in Buddhist Animal Ethics," *Journal of Buddhist Ethics* 21 (2014): 623–655, points to the tension between the categorical rejection of violence towards animals, and the excruciatingly violent punishments promised for those who violate this precept.

22. Jackson, *The Mongols and the Islamic World,* 300.

23. See Prazniak, "Ilkhanid Buddhism," 675.

24. Richard Folz, *Animals in Islamic Tradition and Muslim Cultures* (London: Oneworld, 2014), 88.

25. See Helmut Ritter, ed., *Die dogmatischer Lehren der Anhänger des Islam,* 2nd ed. (Wiesbaden: Franz Steiner Verlag, 1963), 254–255.

26. Yosef Qafih, ed. and trans., *Sefer ha-Nivḥar bi-Emunot ve-De'ot* (Jerusalem: Sura, 1970), 145.

27. Shlomo Pines, trans., *Moses Maimonides: The Guide of the Perplexed* (Chicago: University of Chicago Press, 1963), 468.

28. 'Abd al-Salām Hārūn, ed., *Kitāb al-ḥayawān* (Cairo: al-Bābī al-Ḥalabī, 1938–1945), vol. 3, 392–397.

29. Ṣadr al-Din al-Shirāzī, *al-Ḥikma al-Muta'āliyya fī al-Asfār al-Arba'a* (Beirut: Dar Ehia al-Tourath al-Arabi, 2002), vol. 8, 233–241, at 240; I owe the reference to Eiyad S. Al-Kutubi, *Mulla Sadra and Eschatology: Evolution of Being* (London: Routledge, 2014), 83n16. Some segments of this discussion are translated and discussed in Shlomo Pines, "La conception de la conscience de soi chez Avicenne et chez Abu'l-Barakât al-Baghdâdî," *Archives d'histoire doctrinale et littéraire du moyen âge* 21 (1954): 21–98, at 54 and especially note 1; however, the question of an immaterial soul for animals does not come up in the text presented by Professor Pines.

30. David Reisman, *Mubāḥathāt: The Making of the Avicennan Tradition: The Transmission, Contents, and Structure of Ibn Sīnā's Al-Mubāḥathāt (The Discussions)* (Leiden: Brill, 2002).

31. al-Shirāzī, *al-Ḥikma al-Muta'āliyya,* 233; on Mulla Ṣadra's references to the *Mubāḥathāt* as *murāsalāt,* see Reisman, *Mubāḥathāt,* 144n94.

32. Sabine Schmidtke, "The Doctrine of the Transmigration of Soul According to Shihāb al-Dīn al-Suhrawardī (killed 587/1191) and His Followers," *Studia Iranica* 28 (1999): 237–254, at 248–250.

33. John Walbridge, *The Wisdom of the Mystic East: Suhrawardi and Platonic Orientalism* (Albany: State University of New York Press, 2001), 80.

34. John Walbridge, "The Science of Mystic Lights: Quṭb al-Dīn Shīrāzī and the Illuminationist Tradition in Islamic Philosophy" (Ph.D. diss., Harvard University, 1992), 145–147.

35. See also B. Carra de Vaux's entry "Tanāsukh" in the first edition of the *Encyclopedia of Islam,* vol. 4 (Leiden: Brill, 1934), 648–649, for hadith relating that men are turned into animals or resurrected in forms of animals.

36. See Serafina Cuomo, *Pappus of Alexandria and the Mathematics of Late Antiquity* (Cambridge: Cambridge University Press, 2007), chap. 2.

37. See Abdelhamid I. Sabra, "The Andalusian Revolt Against Ptolemaic Astronomy: Averroes and al-Bitruji," in *Transformation and Tradition in the Sciences: Essays in honor of I. Bernard Cohen,* ed. Everett Mendelsohn (Cambridge: Cambridge University Press, 1984), 133–153.

38. See, e.g., the index to William C. Chittick, *The Sufi Path to Knowledge* (Albany: State University of New York Press, 1989), 458, s.v. *khuluq,* for four variations in the formula; for a different, comparative perspective, see Nancy Roberts, "Imitatio Christi, Imitatio Muhammadi, Imitatio Dei," *Journal of Ecumenical Studies* 47 (2012): 227–248.

39. Though Ibn Kammūna cites here the Torah explicitly, he may have had in mind as well the verse from Luke 6:36, "You must be compassionate, just as your Father is compassionate," which surely echoes the Jewish homily cited above.

40. See Walbridge, *Wisdom of the Mystic East,* 55.

41. Hermann Landolt, "Ghazali and 'Religionswissenschaft,'" *Recherches en spiritualité iranienne: recueil d'articles* (Tehran: University of Tehran Press, 1991), 25–81, at 33n59.

42. See Alexander Altmann and Samuel M. Stern, *Isaac Israeli: A Neoplatonic Philosopher of the Early Tenth Century* (Chicago: University of Chicago Press, 2010), 196–208.

43. The term is discussed extensively by Henri Corbin, *En Islam iranien* (Paris: Gallimard, 1971), vol. 2, chap. 1; great scholar though he was, Corbin's disquisitions must be read with caution. It was applied notably with reference to Mulla Ṣadra; see Reza Pourjavady, *Philosophy in Early Safavid Iran: Najm al-Dīn Maḥmūd al-Nayrīzī and His Writings* (Leiden: Brill, 2011), 94.

44. On Ibn Kammūna's problem with his eyesight, see Reza Pourjavady and Sabine Schmidtke, *A Jewish Philosopher of Baghdad* (Leiden: Brill, 2006), 15n80.

45. However, as Pourjavady and Schmidtke, *Jewish Philosopher,* 95, note, the autograph copy (present whereabouts unknown) is dated one year later.

II. On Practice, Second Gate: Translation

1. Aristotle, *Politics* 1.1253a.

2. See the Arabic text in Reza Pourjavady and Sabine Schmidtke, *A Jewish Philosopher of Baghdad* (Leiden: Brill, 2006), 176, l. 4 and notes 567, 568. The manuscripts give a number of options, all using the *mufā'ala* form; I choose the pair that fits the context best, *muqāraḍa* (a

share in profits of a loan) and *muʿāwaḍa* (in legal jargon, "do ut des," an understanding that something will be done and something given in return).

3. This chapter is obviously gendered, the assumption being that the head of the household, who is the recipient of Ibn Kammūna's advice, is a male.

4. The "rule" that has been mentioned must refer to the general advice given in the preceding chapter, while the "branches," that is, the topics and subtopics, should refer to more specific instruction regarding particular areas to be cared for, much as we speak of the branches of government; in Islamic law, the branches are the different chapters in a law manual, each covering a specific area of concern.

5. Someone who cannot obey the dictates of his own conscience should not expect others to heed his instructions.

6. When severe punishment has been decreed, the ruler faces a dilemma. If the punishment is too harsh, then the ruler has committed a great injustice to the convict; but should the ruler recant, his credibility would be damaged. Hence the advice is to avoid meting out very severe punishments; then the ruler can insist that they be carried out without doing undue harm to the convict or to his own reputation for justice.

7. For more about this folk saying see the Synopsis and Commentary.

8. This paragraph, "He ought not to neglect matters of religion . . . the king is its guard" (178, ll. 1–7) follows closely al-Māwardī's advice in two different places in *Tashīl al-Naẓar wa-Taʿjīl al-Ẓafar*, ed. Riḍwān al-Sayyid (Beirut: Dar al-Nahdah al-Arabiyyah, 1981). Lines 1–3, which urge the ruler not to neglect affairs of religion, are found in almost the same wording in *Tashīl*, 248. Lines 3–7 then present six principles of statecraft, two of them more fundamental, followed by four virtues. These are exactly the same principles listed in

Tashīl, 275, though again al-Māwardī goes to much greater length in elaborating them.

9. The Arabic *raghba,* which I have rendered "desire," has here the sense of a strong intention or aim, an intense motivation or craving which radiates upon one's surroundings. For further discussion on this word, see the Synopsis and Commentary, and note 10 in the preceding section.

10. The Arabic has *tawfīr al-amwāl;* literally, the ruler's policies lead to "the increase in funds [or "properties"]."

11. This opening sentence is found word for word in al-Māwardī, *Tashīl,* 280, cited from "one of the rhetoricians." Accordingly, I follow the variants recorded in notes 608 and 609 of Pourjavady and Schmidtke, *Jewish Philosopher,* 178, choosing *ifḍāl,* which I render here "patronage." See the Synopsis and Commentary for further discussion.

12. This sentence too is found nearly word for word in al-Māwardī, *Tashīl,* 61. On the weighty political influence exercised by some members of the harem, see Nadia Maria El-Cheikh, "The *qahramâna* in the Abbasid Court: Position and Functions," *Studia Islamica* (2003): 41–55; El-Cheikh, "Caliphal Harems, Household Harems: Baghdad in the Fourth Century of the Islamic Era," in *Harem Histories: Envisioning Places and Living Spaces,* ed. Marilyn Booth (Durham, N.C.: Duke University Press, 2010), 87–103. Al-Māwardī wrote during the period studied by El-Cheikh; Ibn Kammūna apparently knew that the advice was still pertinent some three hundred years later.

13. Concerning the division into concealed and manifest goods, see the dissertation of Mohammad Yaqub Khan, "A Political Study of al-Mawardi with Special Reference to the Concept of Legitimacy" (Ph.D. diss., University of Leeds, 2001), 115–116. The king will benefit more from a robust economy, in which goods and bullion are in continuous circulation, than from a fattened treasury, where the freezing of assets leads to economic stagnation.

14. Following up on the preceding sentence, this statement adds that when the king builds a reputation for keeping officials for short periods only, those whom he appoints, knowing their tenure will be short, will take as much as possible, as quickly as possible.

15. Pourjavady and Schmidtke, *Jewish Philosopher,* 179, ll. 8–9: *Man khāfa sharraka afsada amraka.* This saying is attributed to the Persian king Anushirwān in al-Māwardī, *Tashīl,* 327; it is included in many gnomologies. I have already noted that manuals of statecraft of the sort Ibn Kammūna is likely to have drawn upon are considered to present a mix of Persian and Islamic materials.

16. The advice not to favor the Muslim over the *dhimmī* is in line with the *yasa* promulgated by Chinggis Khan; see the Synopsis and Commentary. See also below, note 20.

17. The Arabic *madhhab* may mean school of thought, doctrine, creed, ideology, and the like.

18. Literally, "when the fundamental constituents (*mādda*) are not severed, it may harm even a great king." Ibn Kammūna is using here the terminology of medical pathology.

19. For further discussion of this interesting passage on prayer, see the Synopsis and Commentary.

20. For another saying attributed to the "people of experience," see below, note 23. As far as I know, this is not a hadith.

21. See the Synopsis and Commentary for further discussion of this maxim.

22. Justice is used here in the sense of giving each thing its due; and this is what happens in the healthy functioning of the human body.

23. In this case it seems that by "masters of experience" Ibn Kammūna has in mind chroniclers, especially those recording noteworthy episodes from the histories of rulers. Specifically, he is referring to the following story, recorded in *Adāb al-Sulṭāniyyāt,* and cited here from Henry H. Howorth, *History of the Mongols from the Ninth*

to the Nineteenth Century (London: Longmans, Green, 1876), part 1, p. 202: "When the master of Baghdad Khulagu proposed this question to the Muhammedan doctors: 'Which is preferable: A just sovereign who is an unbeliever, or a true believer who is unjust;' they agree that the just infidel was preferable to the unjust Mussulman."

24. In translating "the extraordinary inspirations that have been created in" I follow the variant in Pourjavady and Schmidtke, *Jewish Philosopher,* 183n689, "*khuliqa fī.*"

25. Ibn Kammūna's close attention to the question of whether animals possess souls is noteworthy; see the Synopsis and Commentary for a lengthy analysis.

26. "Autonomous" in the sense of being the highest in the chain of authority—king, khan, or whatever—and hence not dependent or answerable to someone who holds a higher position.

27. "Reigning order" is my approximate (and unsure) rendering of *al-amr al-aghlab;* it denotes, as I see it, the established and accepted rules for conducting oneself, matters of protocol, and the like.

28. This Muslim formula, with its Shi'a overtones, constitutes no proof for Ibn Kammūna's conversion. The *Kalimāt* was written for a Muslim patron and, given the "Abrahamic" nature of this treatise, Ibn Kammūna could in all sincerity sign off with a blessing to the Prophet of Islam and his descendants.

Index

Baghdad, 1, 2, 3, 4
Bahā' al-Dīn al-Juwaynī, 4, 8, 9, 131, 149
Baḥya Ibn Paquda, 92
Bar Hebraeus, 97
Being, Necessary. *See* Necessary Being
Beliefs and Opinions (Saadya), 142
Benjamin of Tudela, 132
Bible, Hebrew, 25, 97, 140. *See also individual books*
al-Bidāya wa-l-Nihāya (Ibn Kathīr), 135
al-Bīrūnī, 19
bodies, heavenly, 59, 101
Buddhism, Buddhist, 7, 60–62, 140, 144

cause, first (divine), 22, 23, 32, 40, 47
Chinggis Khan, 7, 139
Christianity, 5, 6, 7, 28
Collection (Pappus of Alexandria), 145
compound, 26, 39, 42–46, 56, 57, 63, 77, 78, 80, 100. *See also* animals: compounds; simple
conversion, 7–8, 141
cosmos, 20–21, 28, 32, 39, 46, 69, 102, 139, 160; cosmology, 27, 146; governor of, 28, 38, 45; intellectual, 85; unity of, 30; workings of, 15
creation, 20, 25, 42, 45, 113, 117, 120, 121: interaction with, 139, 159; in time, 23; of man, 81; secrets of, 160
Creator, 64; goodness of, 48
Cuzari (ha-Levi), 5

Davidson, Herbert, 107
Dawlatshāh b. Sanjar al-Ṣāḥibī, 3–4
deity, 20, 22, 24, 30, 32, 38, 40, 148; characteristics, 17–18, 25–27, 29, 41, 46, 98, 139; contemplation, 28; knowledge of, 4; most perfect, 28; relationship with humans, 19, 24, 99, 102, 104. See also *al-mūjid;* Necessary Being; Supreme Being; *wujūd: wājib al-wujūd*
desire, 19, 86, 98, 100, 125, 135–136, 155, 156, 158; object of, 28, 44
dhāt (essence), 31, 42, 61, 65, 77, 99; root essence (*dhāt aṣliyya*), 78; very essence (*nafs al-dhāt*), 79
dhāt (self, his [own]), 31, 45, 61, 99
dhawq (taste), 70
dhikr, 95, 111
dhimmi, dhimma, 8, 132, 137–139, 157–158
dissolution (*inḥilāl*), 58, 80
divine, 19, 29, 30, 99, 103–106, 117, 120, 141; attributes, 17, 36, 98, 105, 115; benefits, 124; conception of, 17; decree, 23, 119; divine-like, 47–48, 148, 163; entity, 24; essence, 65; guidance, 67; inspired, 145, 147; kindness, 103, 120, 125;